INSIGHT **COMPACT** GUIDES

PRAGUE

```
D1541168
```

Compact Guide: Prague is the ultimate easy-reference guide to this jewel in the Bohemian crown. It tells you all you need to know about Prague's great attractions, from the Castle to the Lesser Quarter, from the Charles Bridge to the Old Town Square.

This is just one title in *Apa Publications'* new series of pocket-sized, easy-to-use guidebooks intended for the independent-minded traveller. Based on an award-winning formula pioneered in Germany, *Compact Guides* pride themselves on being up-to-date and authoritative. They are in essence mini travel encyclopedias, designed to be comprehensive yet portable, both readable and reliable.

Star Attractions

An instant reference
to some of Prague's
most popular tourist
attractions to help
you on your way.

Prague Castle p19

Golden Lane p30

National Gallery p35

Loreto Church p37

Loreto Treasury p38

Strahov Monastery p38

Waldstein Palace p42

Charles Bridge p46

*Astronomical
Clock p49*

Jewish Quarter p54

Karlstein Castle p70

Prague

Introduction

Places

Culture

Leisure

Practical Information

Prague – The Golden City

Even the moon assured the great Czech writer Jan Neruda that 'no other city can compare with the beauty of Prague', whilst for Paul Valéry there was 'no other place in the world where the magnificence of the whole is subordinated to so many precious details and cameos'. Virtually no other city has been praised across the centuries as continuously and effusively as Prague. 'Prague the Golden' and 'Prague of the Hundred Towers' are just two of its epithets, which seem as fitting now as they were in days long past.

Anybody who gazes over the city from the parapets of Hradčany Castle must surely appreciate why. Prague is the most fortunate of all European cities; fortunate because its skyline was never touched by the ravages of war and because its essential appearance was never scarred by the addition of modern eyesores. Viewed from the Castle Hill, the historical centre, whose hundreds of rooftops reflect the golden patina of the midday sun, clings to the gently curving bend in the River Vltava (also called the Moldau). Its banks seem to be only just held together by the filigreed constructions of its bridges: on the one side lies the Lesser Quarter and on the other the Old Town.

The Old Clock Tower

5

The geography of Prague

Prague/Praha, the capital of the Czech Republic, is situated on the River Vltava, spread out between seven hills. It lies between 176–397m (575–1,300 ft) above sea level, at 50° North and 14° East; about the same latitude as Frankfurt, Land's End and Vancouver. The city has a population of 1.3 million living over a total area of 497 sq km (190 sq miles). Historic Prague boasts over 500 towers and steeples, and the city's parks and gardens cover a total area of 870 hectares (2,150 acres).

The spires of Prague

It is not difficult to find your bearings in Prague, especially as the most important sights can be reached on foot. The city's small centre (Prague 1) is divided into the historic quarters of Malá Strana (Lesser Quarter), Staré Město (Old Town), and Nové Město (New Town). The latter is centred around Wenceslas Square and extends to a street called Na príkope. Adjacent and to the north is the Staré Město, which extends across the Old Town Square (Staroměstské náměstí) and the right bank of the Vltava and the Charles Bridge. The picturesque Malá Strana lies on the left of the river. Two other self-contained districts are the Josefov (Jewish Quarter) and Hradčany, the Castle Quarter.

Prague is divided into a total of 56 districts which are administered from town halls. The city possesses a university and 11 colleges of higher education (the figures in brackets refer to the year of foundation or reformation):

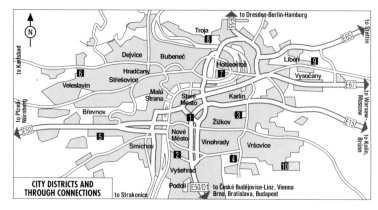

the Charles University (1348), the Institute of Technology (1707), the Institute of Agriculture (1952), the Institute of Chemistry and Technology (1952), the School of Business Studies (1953), the Academy of Music (1811, 1945), the Academy of Fine Arts (1799, 1887), the Academy of Applied Arts (1885, 1946) and two theological faculties. The oldest of the city's many secondary schools is the Academic Grammar School (1556). The first girls' grammar school was founded in 1890.

Summer in the city

Climate

Prague's climate is characterised by fairly mild winters and moderately warm summers. From a climatic point of view, the best times to visit Prague are the spring and autumn. May, when the parks and gardens are in full bloom, heralds the classic music festival, Prague Spring, while the mild autumn with its stable weather offers the best prospects for extended strolls around town.

The Czech Republic

Prague is the seat of the national president and the National Assembly of the Czech Republic. On 1 January 1993 the federal state of Czechoslovakia ceased to exist. The revolution which swept the country in 1989 brought the old quarrels between the two republics once again to the forefront, and strong political movements in both republics negotiated the division of the country during the course of 1992. The Czech Republic has opted to go for more rapid change under a programme of economic reforms based on the principle of the free market, and is making enormous efforts to establish the conditions under which it will participate actively in the European Community of the future.

Geography

The Czech Republic encompasses an area of 78,864 sq km (30,450 sq miles) and has common borders with Germany,

Austria and Poland. In the west and north the border of the region is defined by the Bohemian Forest (Český les and Šumava), the Ore Mountains (Krušné hory) and the Giant Mountains (Krkonoše), whose highest point is the Schneekoppe (Sněžka; 1,602m/5,126ft).

The principal river flowing through Moravia, the province on the eastern borders of Bohemia, is the March (Morava). The Oder (Odra) rises in northern Moravia. In the east lie the Lesser Carpathians. The Czech Republic is linked to the North Sea, the Baltic and the Black Sea by the Elbe, the Oder and the Danube.

Population

The population of the republic is over 10 million, and while the majority are ethnic Czechs, there remains a sizeable German minority.

Industry and trade

Czech industry has made great progress since World War II, particularly in the spheres of mechanical engineering and iron and steel production. Approximately 10 percent of industry is centred in and around the capital. Apart from these three major industries, the Czech Republic also manufactures textiles, shoes, wood products and glass, for which Bohemia has always been renowned. The mechanical engineering industry is heavily export-oriented; the major markets are in eastern and southeastern Europe. Since 1988, joint ventures with foreign companies have been permitted, and many of these are now flourishing.

Administration

The country is divided into seven regions (*Kraje*), plus the metropolitan district of Prague. The regions are subdivided into districts.

Bohemian glass

An official engagement

Folk music in the Old Town

Historical Highlights

The region in which Prague stands today was inhabited during the Stone Age.

In c 400BC the area was invaded by a Celtic tribe, the Boii, who gave Bohemia its name. During the 4th and 5th centuries AD they were joined by the migrating Slavs. During the 7th century, the territory was ruled over by an enterprising Frankish merchant named Samo, who established the first state on Bohemian soil.

From the 9th until the 14th century, Bohemia was ruled without interruption by princes from the Přemyslid dynasty. Prince Bořivoj I is thought to have been baptised by the Slavic apostle Methodius in 873. The first Prague Castle was built.

921–35 Prince Wenceslas (Václav) is murdered by his brother Boleslav I. St Wenceslas later becomes the patron saint of Bohemia.

965 The Jewish merchant Abraham Ben Jacob (Ibrahim Ibn Jakub) provides the first recorded description of the city of Prague, 'built of stone and limestone', adding that it was the 'largest trading city in those lands'.

973 The founding of the bishopric of Prague.

1085 Prince Vladislav is proclaimed the first king of Bohemia by Emperor Henry IV.

1140–72 Rule of Prince Vladislav II, who becomes King Vladislav I in 1158. He founds Strahov Monastery and has the first stone bridge – the Judith Bridge – built across the Vltava.

1173–78 Prince Soběslav II. Equal rights are afforded to the Germans, who continue to arrive in ever-increasing numbers. Special privileges awarded to German merchants.

1197–1230 King Přemysl Otakar I. Emperor Frederick II confirms and extends the privileges of the Bohemian kings. The throne becomes hereditary; under Wenceslas I (Václav I) the Old City is enlarged and fortified.

1253–78 Under Přemysl Otakar II Bohemia becomes a major power by conquering most of Austria. In 1257 the Lesser Quarter is granted a town charter. Otakar is killed in 1278 in the Battle of the Marchfeld against Rudolf von Habsburg.

1306 The murder of the 17-year-old King Wenceslas II (Václav) of Bohemia marks the end of the male line of the Přemyslids.

1310–46 King John of Luxembourg, son of the Emperor Henry VII. Married to the Premyslid Princess Elizabeth, he founds the Luxembourg dynasty and begins the construction of the Cathedral. Prague becomes an archbishopric in 1344.

1346–78 King Charles I (from 1355 Emperor Charles IV). During his reign Prague experiences its most glittering Golden Age and becomes the largest city in Central Europe. Charles founds the university in 1348 and has the New Town laid out. The most important Gothic buildings in the city are built or at least started. The Golden Bull (1356) confirms the rights and internal autonomy of Bohemia. Peter Parler carves Charles IV in stone on the triforium of St Vitus' Cathedral.

1378–1419 King Wenceslas IV, the son of Charles IV. In 1393 he has the Vicar General, John of Nepomuk, thrown into the Vltava from the Charles Bridge. During his reign Jan Hus becomes rector of the university and preaches in the Czech language at the Bethlehem Chapel. He comes into conflict with the Catholic Church establishment, and in 1415 is burnt at the stake in Constance. In 1400 the Electoral Princes depose Wenceslas, whose support of the Czechs prompts the German professors and students to move to Leipzig in 1409 and to found the university there.

1419–36 The Hussite Wars. On 30 July 1419, rebellious Hussites led by Jan Zelivsky throw members of the King's Council from a window of the Town Hall in the New Town (The First Defenestration of Prague). After the death of King Wenceslas the Czechs refuse to acknowledge the claim to the throne of his brother, the Emperor Sigismund. At the Battle of Vitkov near Prague on 14 July 1420, the Hussites under Jan Žižka manage to repel the emperor's armies.

As a result of the Four Articles of Prague (1420), which demand amongst other things the celebration of the Holy Communion *sub utraque specie* ('in both kinds', i.e. in bread and wine), a schism develops amongst the Hussite supporters, forming two camps: the moderate Utraquists, based in Prague and the radical Taborites, based in the city of Tabor. In 1433 the Prague Hussites agree on a compromise with the Catholic Church. In 1436 Sigismund is recognised as King of Bohemia, only to die a year later.

1458–71 King George of Poděbrady (Jirí z Podřbrad), leader of the Utraquists, later known as the 'Hussite King'. George of Poděbrady is succeeded in 1471 by the Jagiellon kings of Poland: Vladislav II (1471–1516) and Louis (1516–26). Following the latter's death in the battle of Mohacs in Southern Hungary, the throne of Bohemia and Hungary passes to the Habsburgs, who subsequently rule Bohemia until 1918. The first kings of the new dynasty are Ferdinand I (1526–64) and Maximilian II (1564–76).

1576–1612 Emperor Rudolf II. During his reign, Prague becomes the imperial residence once more, experiencing a second Golden Age. Famous artists and scientists from all over Europe work for the king. His gallery of paintings was supposed to outdo all others. With his 'Letter of Majesty' (1609) he grants the Bohemian estates freedom of religious worship. He is succeeded by his brother Matthias (1611–19).

1618–48 The Thirty Years' War. The Second Defenestration of Prague, where the two governors of Bohemia and their secretary are thrown out of the Council Room window at Hradčany, takes place on 23 May 1618 following the violation of the 'Letter of Majesty'. The event unleashes the Bohemian War, which develops into the Thirty Years' War. The leader of the Protestant Union, Elector Frederick V of the Palatinate, is appointed King of Bohemia (1619).

Under Frederick's leadership the Bohemian and Moravian estates are defeated on 8 November 1620 in the Battle of the White Mountain by the Catholic forces under Duke Maximilian of Bavaria. Frederick, the 'Winter King', flees to the Netherlands. On the orders of Emperor Ferdinand II, the 27 leaders of the 1618 uprising are executed on 21 June 1621 in front of the Old Town Hall. Some 150,000 Bohemian Protestants go into exile.

The country becomes Catholic once again, and is ruled by a new aristocracy loyal to the emperor. In 1648, Swedish troops under General Königsmark occupy Hradčany Castle and the Lesser Quarter, but fail to capture the Old Town. After their withdrawal, the process of reconversion to Catholicism continues.

1680 Uprising of Bohemian peasants against the feudal system of government. Catholic and German dominance of spiritual life becomes more all-embracing. At the same time, baroque art reaches its zenith.

1711–40 Emperor Charles VI. The Counter-Reformation gains greater influence; more people leave the country.

1740–80 Maria Theresa. During the War of Austrian Succession (1740–48), the armies of Bavaria, Saxony and France capture Prague in 1741. In 1744 Prussian troops besiege the city. In 1757, during the Seven Years' War, Prague is subjected to attack by the Prussians for more than seven weeks, but the siege is lifted following Frederick the Great's defeat at Kolín. When hostilities come to an end, Maria Theresa has the damage repaired and Prague Castle extended.

1780–90 Emperor Joseph II. The last vestiges of Bohemian self-government disappear. Serfdom is abolished in Bohemia in 1781. The Jews are awarded civic rights. In 1784 the administrations of the hitherto more or less independent towns of Hradčany, the Lesser Quarter, the Old Town and the New Town as well as the Jewish quarter, now known as Josefov, are amalgamated under a single magistrature.

1792–1835 Emperor Francis II (from 1804 Francis I of Austria). During the Napoleonic Wars the country is overrun on several occasions by French and Russian troops; freedom movements continue to be repressed. Rapid industrial expansion makes Bohemia and Moravia the most profitable economic region in the Habsburg empire.

1835–48 Emperor Ferdinand I. Chancellor Metternich continues the repressive course in Bohemia. Growing tensions with Czechs demanding parity of their language with German and the establishment of movements against absolutism and centralism. But the Czechs want nothing to do with the united Germany as envisioned by the German Nationalist Movement.

1848 Under the leadership of the historian Frantisek Palacky, a Slavic Congress assembles in Prague. The Whit Uprising of the Czech working class, students and artisans is brutally crushed by Prince Windischgraetz, and his Austrian forces.

1848–1916 Emperor Francis Joseph I. The war between Prussia and Austria of 1866, fought primarily on Bohemian soil, ends in the Peace of Prague (23 August 1866). Austria and the Bohemian lands withdraw from the German Alliance. Universal suffrage is introduced in Bohemia in 1907. This period sees a renaissance of Czech cultural life in Prague, embodied in the construction of the National Theatre and National Museum. The great Czech composers Smetana, Dvořák and Janaček emerge onto the world music stage.

1914–18 World War I. The estrangement between Czechs and Germans intensifies as the sympathies of the Czechs lie on the side of the Entente Powers and the Germans support the Central Powers. In London, Paris and Washington TG Masaryk, Eduard Beneš, General Stefanik and others work towards the creation of Czechoslovakia.

1918 After the collapse of Austria-Hungary, the Republic of Czechoslovakia is proclaimed on 28 October in Prague. Tomás G Masaryk becomes the first president.

1935 After the resignation of Masaryk (d 1937) at the age of 85, Edvard Benes, previously Foreign Minister, becomes President.

1938 The Munich Agreement between Czechoslovakia, France, Britain, Italy and Germany cedes the Sudetenland to Germany. Benes is succeeded in office by Emil Hácha.

1939 President Hácha is forced to capitulate to Hitler in Berlin (15 March). The Reich Protectorate of Bohemia and Moravia is proclaimed, and German troops occupy the country. Konstantin Baron von Neurath becomes the Reichsprotector.

1939–45 World War II. On 27 September 1941 Neurath is replaced Reinhard Heydrich, second-in-command of the SS. In 1942, Heydrich is assassinated. Those responsible are eventually killed in the Church of St Carlo Borromeo, and the village of Lidice is exterminated. Of the Jewish community of almost 40,000 in Prague, 36,000 are murdered by the Nazis.

On 5 May 1945 rebellion breaks out in Prague. Four days later the city is occupied by the Red Army. Beneš becomes President again. Some 3.5 million Sudeten Germans are dispossessed and deported. More than 240,000 die in the process.

1948 Czechoslovakia becomes a People's Republic. On 7 June Beneš resigns (d. 3 September 1948). He is succeeded by Klement Gottwald.

1960 A new constitution proclaims the transition from People's Republic to Socialist Republic.

1968 Alexander Dubček becomes Secretary General of the Communist Party of Czechoslovakia (KPC); Ludvig Svoboda becomes President. The policy 'Socialism with a human face' encounters the disapproval of the Soviet Union and other members of the Warsaw Pact. On 21 August troops from five member states invade the country.

1969 Czechoslovakia becomes a Federal State on 1 January. On 17 April Dubcek is replaced by Gustáv Husák as party chief.

1975 Husák becomes President of Czechoslovakia as well as secretary-general of the party.

1977 Foundation of a civil rights group known as 'Charter 77' following the Helsinki Accords.

1989–90 Mass demonstrations and a general strike in November and December 1989 (the Velvet Revolution) lead to the resignation of the government, the introduction of a democratic multiparty system and the repeal of the Communist Party's right to participate in government. The dramatist and leader of the newly created Civic Forum, Václav Havel, becomes president. In April 1990 the country's name is changed to Czech and Slovak Federal Republic.

1992 In June elections, the ods (Czech Democratic People's Party), under the leadership of Václav Klaus, wins a majority in Bohemia and Moravia. In Slovakia, the strongest party is the HZDS (Movement for a Democratic Slovakia), under the leadership of Vladimir Meciar, which has campaigned for independence. On 17 July Slovakia declares its independence; Havel resigns from office. Negotiations for the division of Slovak and Czech lands are completed by December.

1 January 1993 The Czech and Slovak Republics become independent, sovereign states.

1993 Václav Havel is re-elected President of the Czech Republic. Alexander Dubček dies of injuries resulting from a car crash.

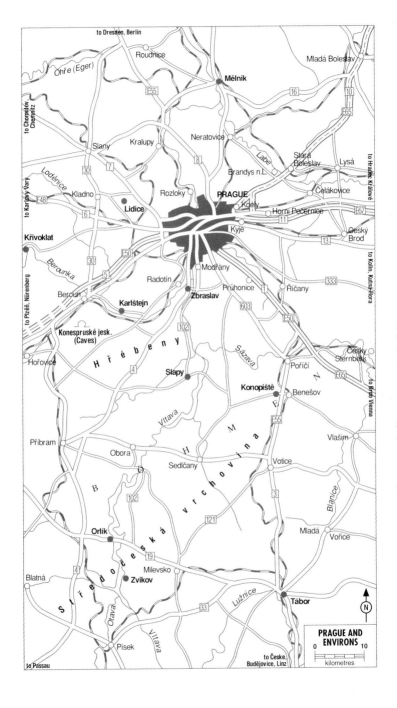

PRAGUE AND
ENVIRONS

0   10

kilometres

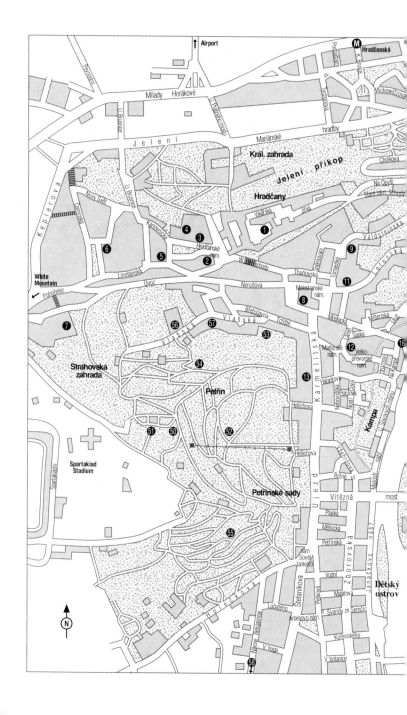

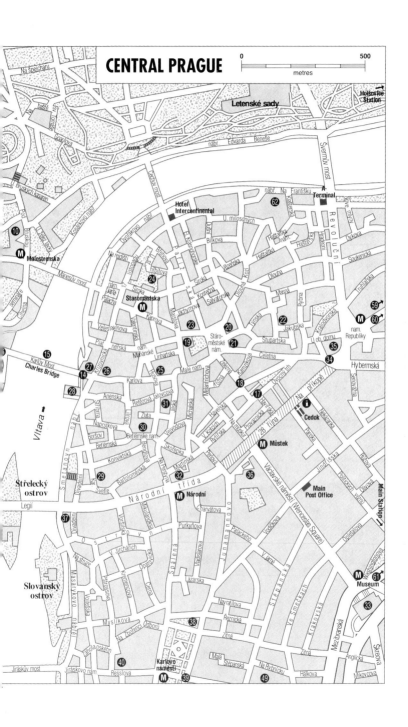

CENTRAL PRAGUE

0   500
metres

Route 1

★★★ Prague Castle and Hradčany

On the ascent to the castle

The name Hradčany refers to the entire district stretching approximately from Prague Castle (Pražský hrad) **1** to the former Strahov Monastery **7** (*see Route 2*). There are a number of different ways of getting to the extensive complex of Prague Castle – one of them a road accessible to cars.

1. By Metro the castle can be approached from the north. From Wenceslas Square, the location of a number of hotels, you should take the underground (*Line A*) as far as Malostranská station, where by following the Staré zámecké schody uphill you can reach the east end of the castle in about five minutes. Alternatively, if you get out at Hradčanská station, you can walk along the Tychonova ul. to the Belvedere (*see page 33*), through the garden and thence to the North Gate of the castle. You can also take the tram for one stop to the Prašný most and walk for about five minutes along the U prašného mostů to reach the North Gate of the castle, through which you should then pass into the second castle courtyard (*see page 20*). The North Gate of the castle can also be reached directly by tram No 22 from the city centre, boarding in front of the K-Mart department store in the Spálená ul., or in front of the National Theatre. Alternatively, you can turn off to the right in front of the gate and pass through the Castle Garden (with the Spanish Hall, *see page 19*) and thence to the main courtyard, the point from which the route described on page 19 actually begins.

16

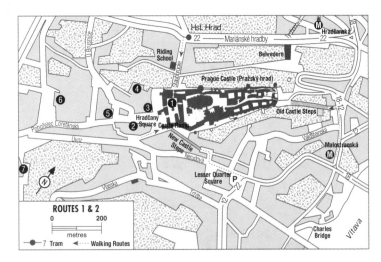

ROUTES 1 & 2
0   200
metres
──●─7 Tram   ◄···· Walking Routes

2. Visitors on foot can choose between two ascents which lead from the Lesser Quarter up to the castle:

a) The climb from the Lesser Quarter Square (Malostranské náměsti) takes about fifteen minutes and leads through the Zámecká ul. and via the Nové zámecké schody to Hradčany Square.

Staré zámecké schody, the Old Castle Steps

b) The Staré zámecké schody begins near the Malostranská underground station and emerges at the east end of the castle. This route is, however, more suitable for the return journey after viewing the castle.

A third approach is to turn from the Lesser Quarter Square (Malostranské náměsti) into the Nerudova ul., then bearing right onto the castle approach ramp (Ke Hradu – closed to all motor vehicles), which leads up to Hradčany Square.

3. If you are travelling by car you should take the Malostranské náměsti and then the Letenská ul., since the Neruda ul. is barred to motor traffic. Following the Klárov, Chotkova ul., Mariáské hradby, Jelení and Keplerova ul., you will eventually come to Pohořelec Square (which can also be reached from the Old Town via the Cechuv Bridge or the Hlákuv Bridge – Veletržni – Milady Horákove – Palackova – Myslbekova – Dlabačov). You should then continue on foot along the Loretánská ul. until you reach Hradčany Square (Hradčanské náměsti).

17

The opening times of the majority of sights are listed below; most are closed on Monday.

The Archbishop's Palace, Hradčany Square

History

The history of Prague Castle is closely linked with that of the city as summarised on pages 8–10.

Nothing remains today of the first wooden fortress built on the bare hill near the ford across the Vltava during the second half of the 9th century. In 1950 remains were discovered of the Church of St Mary, which was built at about the same time; they can be seen at the end of the Castle Gallery [U].

In about 915–20 the Basilica of St George was built [K], which, however, had to be rebuilt after 1142 following a fire. In 926–9, Prince Wenceslas the Saintly erected a small Romanesque round church (rotunda) in honour of St Vitus; it stood on the site which is now occupied by the Wenceslas Chapel [7] of St Vitus' Cathedral [F].

During the 11th and 12th century, the old wooden castle was replaced by a Romanesque building, which today forms the lowest storey of the former Royal Palace (*see page 25*). In 1061–91 a Romanesque basilica was erected in place of the St Vitus Rotunda mentioned above. The remains of this construction can be seen behind the statue of St George [I].

Old Sacristy, St Vitus' Cathedral

Photo opportunity at Hradčany

During the Early Gothic period, i.e. the 13th–14th century, in the reigns of Otakar II, Charles IV and Wenceslas IV, the present middle storey of the former Royal Palace was built. Work started on the construction of St Vitus' Cathedral in 1344. Until 1352 the project was supervised by Matthew of Arras, then until 1399 by Peter Parler and finally by the latter's sons. By this time the choir and its chapels had been completed, as had the Wenceslas Chapel, the eastern section of the nave, the south porch and parts of the south tower.

During the Late Gothic era the former Royal Palace acquired its present upper floor under Vladislav II (1471–1516), including the Vladislav Hall, the castle walls and fortified towers.

When the Habsburg emperor Ferdinand I ascended the throne of Bohemia in 1526, the purely Gothic appearance of the castle underwent rapid changes. Spacious parks and gardens were laid out, and new audience halls and offices as well as the Belvedere pleasure palace [Z] were added. Under Emperor Rudolf II (1576–1612), Prague Castle became the focal point of the empire once more, as it had been during the reign of Charles IV.

It was not until the 18th century, however, that Castle Hill finally lost its medieval appearance. The Empress Maria Theresa ordered the repair and modernisation of the buildings, which had been badly damaged during the Seven Years' War. By filling in the moat on the west side, redesigning the first castle courtyard and erecting a number of buildings linking together existing wings, Hradčany Castle was given its present appearance.

Only St Vitus' Cathedral, which from 1419 had been left untouched apart from a single four-year building phase, had to wait many more years for its completion: work started in 1872 and was not finished until 1929.

A tour of Prague Castle

As is evident from the various routes listed on pages 16–17, one way of viewing Prague Castle is from west (Hradčany Square or the Staub Bridge) to east (Staré zámecké schody). The main sights to be visited will then be the Castle Gallery [U], the Chapel of the Holy Cross [D] with the Cathedral Treasure, St Vitus' Cathedral [F], the former Royal Palace [J], St George's Church [K] and the Golden Lane [N]. You can also start the tour from the opposite end, beginning at the Staré zámecké schody.

Taking in the sights

If you arrive by bus the most convenient tour is one beginning and ending at Hradčany Square. Refer to the plan on this page. It leads from the Entrance Courtyard [A] to the Second Courtyard [C] with the Chapel of the Holy Cross [D], the Third Courtyard [E] with St Vitus' Cathedral [F] and the former Royal Palace [J], St George's Church [K], the Golden Lane [N] and back via the museum in the Mihulka Tower to the Second Courtyard with the Castle Gallery [U], the former Riding School [T] and the Spanish Hall (*see page 16*).

From the Hradčany Square you first enter the **Entrance Courtyard [A]**, also known as the First Courtyard. It was designed by the Viennese architect Nikolaus von Pacassi, who, on instructions from Maria Theresa, had the moat on the west side of the castle filled in and a number of old buildings demolished and new ones erected. The fighting giants at the entrance (replicas since 1912) were sculpted by Ignaz Platzer the Elder

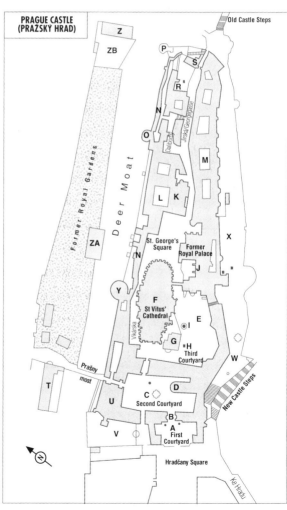

PRAGUE CASTLE
(PRAŽSKÝ HRAD)

Old Castle Steps

Former Royal Gardens

Deer Moat

St. George's Square

Former Royal Palace

St Vitus' Cathedral

Third Courtyard

Second Courtyard

First Courtyard

Hradčany Square

New Castle Steps

Prašný most

Vikářská

Jiřská / Georgsgasse

Ke Hradu

Matthias Gate

Chapel of the Holy Cross

20

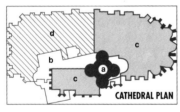

St Vitus' Cathedral

CATHEDRAL PLAN

between 1766–8. The guard is changed every hour on the hour. Integrated into the new buildings, the **Matthias Gate [B]**, dating from 1614, is the oldest secular baroque edifice in Prague; it was the work of Vincenzo Scamozzi, the architect of the New Law Courts in Venice. From the gateway, a staircase on the right leads up to the reception rooms of the President of the Czech Republic.

Behind the gateway is the **Second Courtyard [C]**. This was also completely redesigned by Pacassi during the 18th century. Straight ahead you will see the former **Chapel of the Holy Cross [D]**, built by Anselmo Lurago in 1753. The treasure of St Vitus' Cathedral, previously on display here, is no longer on view. On the left (north) side wall of the Second Courtyard is the entrance to the Castle Gallery [U], described on page 32.

On the way into the Third Courtyard you will pass the lovely baroque fountain, created by Hieronymus Kohl in 1686. There is a post office in the building between the two courtyards; its entrance is in the Third Courtyard.

Opposite the connecting passage to the **Third Courtyard [E]**, the (Neo-Gothic) silhouette of St Vitus' Cathedral soars heavenwards. Together with the new buildings on the south side erected by Pacassi during the 18th century, the cathedral dominates the appearance of the courtyard. If you have sufficient time available, it is worth walking once round the cathedral before entering via the main door, in order to gain a first overall impression of this magnificent example of sacred architecture.

St Vitus' Cathedral (Svatý Vít; daily 9am–5pm) **[F]** was built over the remains of a Romanesque rotunda (926–9) and a Romanesque basilica (1061–96). Construction work was interrupted in 1419 by the Hussite Wars and was not completed until more than 500 years later (in 1929), using the original plans as far as possible and skilfully adding modern building elements. In the adjacent sketch you will also find marked the positions of the Romanesque rotunda of St Vitus' [a], the Romanesque basilica [b], the Gothic section [c] and the Neo-Gothic additions [d].

On the west front of the cathedral (*see Plan, page 21*) is the main entrance **[1]**, with three bronze portals dating from 1927–9. The history of the building of the cathedral from 929–1929 is depicted in the middle; to the left is the legend of St Wenceslas, and to the right that of St Adalbert. The rose window, which has a diameter of 10.4m (33ft), portrays the Creation and is made up of 26,740 separate panes of glass. The interior is 124m (397ft) long, 60m (192ft) wide and 34m (109ft) high; the most notable features are the 21 chapels, which contain a large number of important works of art.

The tour (*see Plan below*) begins on the right-hand side of the nave, passing first of all several Neo-Gothic chapels: the Chapel of St Ludmilla [**2**], the Chapel of the Holy Sepulchre [**3**] and the Thun Chapel [**4**], with modern windows and a number of old tombs. A collection of old manuscripts is kept in the Chapter Library [**5**]. On the right there is the entrance to the South Tower [**6**] (96m/315ft), with a magnificent view of Hradčany and the city (the tower is closed in winter).

Next you will enter the loveliest and most precious section of the cathedral, the **Wenceslas Chapel** [**7**]. This chapel was erected in 1362–7 by Peter Parler above the remains of the Romanesque rotunda.

Wenceslas Chapel

It has been meticulously restored in recent years and houses the tomb of the patron saint of Bohemia, St Wenceslas, as well as relics and a statue (1373). The walls are decorated with semi-precious stones (jasper, amethysts, agate, carnelian, emeralds), and with gold tiles and frescoes. The lower row of frescoes (14th century) depicts the Passion of Christ, while those above (c 1509) portray the legend of St Wenceslas.

Above the chapel, in the Crown Chapel (not open to the public), which has a door with seven locks, the Bohemian coronation insignia have been kept since 1625.

Beside the Wenceslas Chapel begins the ambulatory, which is the oldest part of the cathedral.

On the right lie, in succession, the Martinitz Chape [**8**] and the Chapel of the Holy Cross [**9**]. From the

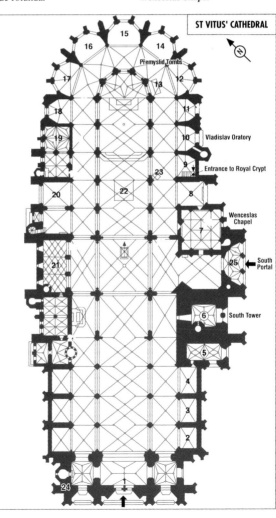

ST VITUS' CATHEDRAL

Přemyslid Tombs

Vladislav Oratory

Entrance to Royal Crypt

Wenceslas Chapel

South Portal

South Tower

Chapel of the Holy Cross

latter, you can enter the Romanesque rooms underneath the cathedral and the Royal Crypt, which was redesigned in 1928–35 (9–11am and 12.30–4pm). Within nine sarcophagi lie Charles IV (centre), Ladislas Postumus (right), George of Poděbrady (left), Wenceslas IV and (facing in the opposite direction) his brother Johann von Görlitz, Rudolf II and Charles IV's four wives. At the end of the crypt, in an Empire-style coffin, lies Archduchess Maria Amalie, the daughter of Empress Maria Theresa, and – in a shared coffin – members of the family of Charles IV. A number of the archaeological discoveries made here are now on view in the Chapel of the Holy Cross, as are the coronation insignia of King Rudolf I of Habsburg.

Before continuing from the Chapel of the Holy Cross through the choir, you should study the Triforium, the passageway under the windows of the main choir. A series of 21 portrait busts stood here until 1983; they represented some of the most important examples of medieval sculpture. All were the work of Peter Parler and his pupils and were produced between 1374 and 1385. The busts include: John of Luxembourg and his wife, Elizabeth of Bohemia; Charles IV and his four wives, Elizabeth of Pomerania, Anna of Schweidnitz, Anne of the Palatinate and Blanche of Valois; Charles' brother John Henry of Moravia and Wenceslas of Luxembourg; Charles' son, later Wenceslas IV and his wife, Johanna of Bavaria. Unfortunately the original busts have been removed from their historical positions, but casts of them can be seen in the former Royal Palace (J) (*see page 25*).

Continuing through the ambulatory, the Chapel of the Holy Cross is followed by the **Vladislav Oratory [10]**, built in 1493 as a gallery and connected by a cloister with the former Royal Palace. Also worth studying is the Late Gothic ribbed vaulting. To the left are two large wooden

Gothic vaulting,
Vladislav Oratory

reliefs carved by Georg Bendl in 1630 and representing the devastation of the cathedral by the Calvinist iconoclasts in 1619.

In the Wallenstein or Mary Magdalene Chapel [**11**] on the right are the tombstones of the architects Matthew of Arras and Peter Parler, discovered in 1928. In the **Chapel of St John Nepomuk** [**12**] you can see the remains of Gothic frescoes, a Late Gothic statue of the Virgin (c 1500) and four silver busts of saints dating from about 1700.

Chapel of St John Nepomuk

Opposite the chapel stands the magnificent Memorial to St John Nepomuk [**13**], designed by Josef Emanuel Fischer von Erlach and executed by the Viennese silversmith Johann Joseph Würth. The design of the figurative decoration was the work of several artists.

The three central choir chapels which now follow house the splendid Gothic tombs of six Bohemian princes and kings of the Přemyslid dynasty. They were commissioned by Emperor Charles IV and executed in 1376–7 by Peter Parler and his pupils.

The Chapel of Relics [**14**]: to the right, Přemysl Otakar I (1197–1230), by Peter Parler himself; to the left, Přemsyl Otakar II (1253–78); remains of Gothic frescoes.

23

Chapel of the Virgin Mary [**15**]: on the right, Břetislav I (1034–55); on the left, Spytihnšv II (1055–61); Relief of Calvary (1621).

Chapel of the Virgin Mary

Chapel of St John the Baptist [**16**]: on the right, Břetislav II (1092–1100); on the left, Bořivoj II (1101–7).

The next chapels are the Archbishops' Chapel [**17**] with a Renaissance tomb dating from 1582; the Chapel of St Anne [**18**], with a silver reliquary plate (1266) and a Late Gothic portrait of the Virgin Mary; the Old Sacristy [**19**], with a painted statue of St Michael (17th century), the painting *The Baptism of Christ* (1722) by Peter Brandl and the net vaulting designed by Peter Parler himself, and – the last of the medieval chapels – the Chapel of St Sigismund [**20**], with a baroque altar (1720) and tombs. Opposite the Chapel of St Anne are two more large-scale wooden reliefs by Georg Bendl, representing the flight of the 'Winter King' Frederick of the Palatinate after the Battle of the White Mountain (1620). Of particular interest is the portrayal of the city at the time.

The organ loft [**21**] was built in 1559–61 by Bonifaz Wohlmuth. He was also responsible for the characteristic roof which caps the South Tower.

In the large marble sarcophagus [**22**] in front of the high altar and above the Royal Crypt lie Ferdinand I, his wife Anne of Bohemia and Hungary and his son Maximilian II. The Renaissance grating dates from 1589. Also of note are the Tomb of Count Schlick [**23**], designed in 1723 by Franz M Kaňka and executed by MB Braun; the gilt figures of the Bohemian patron saint (c 1700) on the crossing; the

Tomb of Ferdinand I

The statue of St George

pulpit (1631) and the contemporary windows (1946–7) at the end of the choir. In a side chapel on the left **[24]** are stained glass windows designed by the Prague art nouveau artist Alphons Mucha.

Passing once more through the Main Entrance [1], you should return to the Third Castle Courtyard [E] (*see Plan, page 19*), and then skirt round the cathedral to the left. You will pass the Old Presbytery (17th century), the Monolith [H] in Mrakotin granite erected in 1928 in memory of the victims of World War I, and a replica of the equestrian statue of St George [I]. The original (1373) by the brothers Georg and Martin von Cluj is one of the most important examples of Gothic statuary; since 1967 it has stood in the Monastery of St George (*see page 29*). Here you will also see the remains of the Romanesque basilica (11th century), protected by a roof.

You will then arrive at the ★ **South Tower [6]** (*see page 21*), the work of Peter Parler, his sons Johann and Wenceslas (14th century), Hans Tirol and Bonifaz Wohlmuth (16th century) and Nicolò Pacassi (18th century).

Together with the south portal and the outside wall of the Wenceslas Chapel [7] (*see page 21*), the tower makes up the most attractive and impressive section of the cathedral: the South Front. It was completed not in Gothic but in Renaissance style; during the 19th century, the main entrance was transferred from the south to the west side of the building.

Designed by Peter Parler, the ★ **South Portal [25]** of the cathedral, also known as the 'Golden Doorway', is a triple-arched arcade, narrowing at the back towards a slender door to allow for the abutting Wenceslas Chapel. The modern, attractive bronze grating with representations

South Portal, bronze grating

of the months of the year was completed in 1954 by sculptor Jaroslav Horejec.

Of particular note is the glass mosaic above the door, produced in 1370–1 by Venetian artists and the first of its kind north of the Alps. It portrays the *Last Judgment*. Apart from glass, small pieces of quartz and other natural stones were employed; the golden effect was achieved by laying thick sheets of gold foil between two stones. To protect the masterpiece from adverse climatic effects, it was covered a few years ago with a layer of artificial resin. Apart from depicting the Biblical scenes of the Resurrection of the Dead and the Last Judgment, the picture also portrays the Virgin Mary, St John the Baptist, the apostles, Charles IV and his wife Elizabeth of Pomerania, as well as the six patron saints of Bohemia.

Above the South Portal lies the Crown Chamber (not open to the public), in which the Bohemian coronation insignia has been preserved since 1625.

The right-hand (south) section of the Third Castle Courtyard includes a wing which – like the Entrance Courtyard [A] (*see page 19*) and the Second Courtyard [C] (*see page 20*) – was designed during the reign of Maria Theresa by Pacassi. The large portico with the balcony (by Ignaz Platzer, 1760–1) today forms the entrance to the Presidential Chancellery. The former **Royal Palace [J]** (April to September: daily except Monday, 9am–4.45pm; October to March: 9am–4pm) is linked to the Pacassi buildings; today the palace includes a Romanesque, an Early Gothic and a Late Gothic storey. The tour begins on the upper floor (Late Gothic), which contains the most attractive rooms.

The Royal Palace

The various sections of the upper floor of the palace are numbered below from 1–11 in (round) brackets. The figures refer to the corresponding numbers on the location plan on this page.

To the side of the palace, a ramp leads down into the former palace courtyard to the Early Gothic central storey. To the right, under the portico designed by Pacassi, is the main entrance. From the antechamber (**1**) turn left, initially into the Green Room (**2**), where, on 23 May 1618, the Bohemian estates assembled shortly before the Second Defenestration of Prague. Continue into the Vladislav Room (**3**), which was newly vaulted in 1490–3, and is adorned with the monogram of Vladislav and the coats of arms of Bohemia, Moravia, Luxembourg, Silesia and Poland.

Returning to the antechamber, the next room on the left is the famous ★★ **Vladislav Audience Hall (4)**, regarded as the finest Late Gothic room in Central Europe.

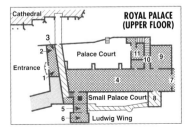

ROYAL PALACE (UPPER FLOOR)

Vladislav Hall

It was built between 1493–1502 by Benedikt Ried as a Throne Room and as a jousting hall; it is 62m (198ft) long, 16m (51ft) wide and up to 13m (42ft) high. In view of the two storeys below, the construction of the vast hall without supporting pillars was a remarkable architectural feat. Of particular note are the artistically interwoven ribs forming the vaulting. Today the national president is elected in the former Throne Room.

At the nearest end of the room you should turn first of all to the right into the so-called Ludwig Wing, which contains the offices of the Bohemian Chancellery. The first room is the Chamber of Scribes and Secretaries (**5**), with the coat of arms of King Ludwig (1516–26) and a model of the castle during the 18th century which clearly shows the cathedral in its unfinished state.

In the Governor's Room (**6**) next door, on 23 May 1618, the imperial governors Martinitz and Slawata and their private scribe Fabricius were thrown from the east (left-hand) window 16m (51ft) into the castle moat below (today the Wallgarten), a deed that precipitated the Thirty Years' War.

On the way back to the Vladislav Hall (*see page 25*) you can ascend via the linking passageway to the Imperial Court Chancellery if it is open, and then across into the Vladislav Oratory in St Vitus' Cathedral (*see page 20*).

In the Vladislav Hall, cross to the opposite (east) side wall. Under a three-section Renaissance window (c 1500) and through a doorway added in 1598, there is a balcony above the Chapel of All Saints (**7**).

Chapel of All Saints

A Gothic chapel was added here on the site of a Romanesque royal chapel; subsequently completed by Peter Parler, it was later destroyed during the great castle fire of 1541, then rebuilt in Renaissance style in 1570–1, and extended as far as the Vladislav Hall and linked to it by means of this doorway.

Of note are the *Descent from the Cross* and a triptych by Hans von Aachen (1552–1615), as well as a twelve-painting picture cycle in the choir dating from 1699, by Christian Dittmann. It shows scenes from the life of St Prokop, who was buried here. On the High Altar is the painting entitled *All Saints* by Wenceslas Lorenz Reinder (1689–1743).

Return once more to the Vladislav Hall and turn left to emerge onto the Observation Terrace (**8**). This affords a very fine view of the town and (to the left) the outside facade of the Chapel of All Saints and the Noblewomen's Convent as well as (to the right) the exterior facade of the Vladislav Hall and the Ludwig Wing, which was extended in 1503–10 by Benedict Ried. The last window on the left is the one from which the Defenestration of Prague took place.

Crossing the Vladislav Hall again, you will then enter the ★ **Old Common Law Chamber** (**9**). Dating from the reign of Wenceslas IV, the room was rebuilt by Benedikt Ried in about 1500 and restored in 1559–63 by Bonifaz Wohlmuth following the Great Fire of 1541. The stone Renaissance gallery for the senior clerk is by Wohlmuth; the furnishings – based on old models – date from the 19th century. The royal throne is on the window side; the archbishop's throne and the benches for the clergy are on the left, whilst the seats of the estates officials and lords temporal are on the right.

On the walls are copies of paintings of Habsburg rulers (18th and 19th century). The sessions of the Bohemian estates were held here until 1847. Today, the national president formally signs the election protocol in this room following his election.

Nearby, the Knights' Staircase (**10**) leads down to the middle storey (see below). Ignore this for now and ascend the spiral staircase to the chancelleries of the Estates Chronicles and the Royal Archives, if they are open. The Estates Chronicles were books in which important resolutions and the ownership status of towns and monasteries and the property owned by important individuals were recorded from the 13th century onwards.

In the small Estates Chancellery Room are tables dating from the 17th century; on the walls are painted the coats of arms of the leading officials.

The Estates Chronicles were kept in the baroque cupboards of the Estates Chancellery Chamber and in a carved wooden cupboard dating from 1562 in the adjacent main Estates Chancellery Room. The Royal Archive was converted into a meeting chamber for the estates authorities in 1737; from 1838–1884 the room housed the Royal Archives, a collection of privileges belonging to the Bohemian crown.

View from the Observation Terrace

Old Common Law Chamber

Nowadays the Estates Chancellery houses a permanent exhibition illustrating the duties of that body.

Returning once again to the Vladislav Hall, you should bear left towards the **Knights' Staircase**, passing en route the New Court of Appeal (**11**) (left).

Knights' Staircase

The staircase was constructed by Benedikt Ried in 1500 and has a magnificent rib vaulted ceiling. It enabled the riders who were to take part in the jousting to ride on horseback from the palace courtyard into the Vladislav Hall.

You should leave the upper storey of the former Royal Palace via the Knights' Staircase, which will bring you to the entrance to the Romanesque lower storey. Descending a steep staircase, you will come to the former South Gate of the Romanesque palace. After passing the remnants of the palace fortifications dating from the 9th century you will enter a room built in about 1140. It is 33m (106ft) long, and leads into another, more recent room housing copies of the sculptures by Peter Parler in St Vitus' Cathedral (*see page 22*).

During World War II the Bohemian crown jewels and a number of valuable works of art from the Cathedral were also stored here.

One of the last rooms on the tour of the exhibition, and one of the most impressive, is the Old Estates Chancellery Chamber, which has a vaulted ceiling supported by two squat pillars. It was built during the 13th century under Přemysl Otakar II and served as the repository for the Estates records, the books in which the properties of the higher estates and the most important resolutions of the Estates Council were recorded.

Two additional interesting rooms which originally formed part of the exhibition are in the so-called Charles Palace. They both date from the 14th century, but are at present not open to the public.

Also closed to the public at present are the extensive excavations underneath the surface of the Third Castle Courtyard, which were dug in the 1920s and which can be reached via an entrance in the rooms of the Charles Palace. Archaeologists discovered remains of the walls of the palace of Wenceslas I (Václav I) dating from about 1250, as well as a watchtower which stood in front. They also found the walls of a small church dedicated to St Bartholomew, the adjoining sacristy with a 13th-century iron grating and a corridor leading to the old Basilica of St Wenceslas containing the graves of priests, and exposed the remains of wooden houses and fortifications.

To the left of the exit from the Pillared Hall of Wenceslas IV, whose slender columns, asymmetric bases of the ribs of the vaulting and wall brackets document the transition to the Late Gothic style, the ramp mentioned above leads up to the Third Courtyard [E] (*see page 20*).

From the lower storey the same staircase leads to the exit at the lower end of the Knights' Staircase. Note the door knocker by the St George's Square exit door.

St George's Basilica

After visiting the former Royal Palace, the tour of the Hradčany continues across Castle Hill. Under the passage linking the palace with the Vladislav Oratory in the Cathedral stands the unadorned west facade of the **Basilica of St George [K]** (Svatélso Jiři). The true character of this, the most important Romanesque building in the city, does not become evident until you step inside. Built in 915–20, the church was reconstructed following a fire in 1142. From 1959–62 it was completely restored and many later additions removed. The triple-naved basilica (April to September: daily except Monday 9am–4.45pm, October to March: 9am–3.45pm) is regarded as the oldest example of Romanesque architecture in Prague. Today the magnificent building serves as a concert hall.

Chapel in St George's Basilica

Worthy of note are the 14th-century tombs of two Dukes of Bohemia: Vratislav I (c 920) on the left and Boleslav II (967–99) on the right. Behind lies the crypt with six slender columns and the most precious masterpiece of Romanesque sculpture in Bohemia: a triple relief created in about 1230 portraying the Virgin Mary with Mlada and Berta – the first abbesses of the Convent of St George – and King Otakar I and his sister Agnes. Also of interest are the raised east choir with an 18th-century double staircase and the remains of Romanesque frescoes (up on the right near the choir), the Chapel of St Ludmilla (14th century) with the Saints' Crypt and St Mary's Chapel (below, to the left of the choir).

To the north of the Basilica of St George stand the former monastery buildings **[L]**, which house a collection of ★ **Old Bohemian Art** (daily except Monday 10am–6pm, entrance beside the basilica).

The collection comprises exhibits from the 14th-18th centuries, including sculptures, reliefs, paintings and altarpieces, including the magnificent six altar panels (c 1380) painted by the Master of Wittingau for the Augustinian monastery of Wittingau in South Bohemia. The panels, considered to represent the summit of Bohemian painting during the 14th century, are painted on both sides: the front was displayed on holy days and the rear on normal days. The front panels depict *Christ on the Mount of Olives*, *The Burial of Christ* and *The Resurrection*; the rear portrays three saints per panel.

The Resurrection

The collection also includes Bohemian paintings and sculptures dating from the baroque era. Amongst them are works by Karel Škréta (1610–74), Michael Willmann (1630–1706), Jan Kupecký (1667–1740), Johann Peter Brandl (1668–1735), Wenzel Lorenz Reiner (1689–1743) and Anton Kern (1710–47).

Continuing along the Jiřská ulice, you should notice on the south facade of the basilica the Renaissance portal, created in 1510–20 by the school of Benedikt Ried. On the right (not open to the public) is the former Convent of Noblewomen [M], built in 1754–5 to a design by Pacassi. A little further on are steps leading down to the Zlatá ulička – ★ **The Golden Lane [N]**, also known as the Goldmakers' or Alchemists' Lane. The 18 tiny, colourfully painted houses were built into the arches of the northern wall to provide housing for minor craftsmen, including goldsmiths. In 1597 they were allocated to the 24 castle guards. (Contrary to popular legend, neither the goldmakers nor the alchemists employed by Rudolf II ever lived here.) Completely renovated in 1952–4, the houses form a sort of open-air museum, and the alley is a popular attraction with visitors from all over the world. The writer Franz Kafka (*see page 77*) lived for a short while at No 22, which is now a tiny museum.

Golden Lane

Above the houses runs a battlement walk (access at the beginning and end of the Golden Lane; closed at the time of going to press). Originally the walk linked the White Tower [O], which served during the 16th and 17th century as state prison and during the 18th century as a debtors' tower for noblemen, with the **Daliborka Tower** [P], a remnant of the Late Gothic castle defences. In 1498 Knight Dalibor, the hero of Bedřich Smetana's opera of the same name (*see page 81*), was held prisoner in the tower, which had been built in 1496 by Benedikt Ried. The only access to his actual cell is a small round opening which can still be seen today. There is a staircase leading down to the Black Tower [S] at the upper end of the Staré zámecké schody.

The Daliborka Tower

From the Golden Lane return to the Jiřská ulice, where you turn to the left. On your right you will see the former Lobkowitz Palace [Q], which has recently been turned into a museum of the history of Bohemia from early times until the revolution in 1848 (daily except Monday 10am–6pm). The exhibits illustrate the history of Bohemia; in the basement is a small exhibition describing the renovation and reconstruction of the building, which was built during the second half of the 16th century in Italian Renaissance style. On the left is the former Office of the Senior Burgrave [R], which was built at about the same time. (The Senior Burgrave was the highest official in Bohemia, whose duty it was to represent the king during the latter's absence.) Today the building is the House of Czech Children. The various rooms were decorated by the country's most important artists.

At the end of Jiřská ulice stands the **Black Tower [S]**, whose origins reach back as far as the 12th century. On the far side, the Staré zámecké schody leads on down towards the River Vltava.

Views from the Black Tower

If you wish to visit the remaining sights on Castle Hill, you should return to the square in front of St George's Church after viewing the Black Tower on the Jiřská ulice. Then you should turn right into the Vikářská ulice, which leads round the northern facade of St Vitus' Cathedral.

There is an information office and a souvenir shop at No 37, called the Mladotův dům. The premises of the former Kapitel Library boast a ceiling decorated with notable frescoes dating from 1725; they are the work of the artist Jan Vodňanský.

Next door, at No 38, is the entrance to the **Mihulka Tower [Y]**, dating from the 13th century. It formed part of the northern fortifications of Prague Castle. Today, the former powder tower houses an interesting museum (daily except Monday 9am–4pm). The exhibition displays examples of Renaissance metal casting and other artefacts, as well as mementoes of the reign of Emperor Rudolf II.

Continuing along the Vikářská ulice, you will eventually come back to the Second Castle Courtyard. On the right-hand side is a passage leading through to the North Gate of the castle and from there across the Prašny most bridge to the former Riding School [T], which was built in about 1694 and between 1947–50 converted into a gallery for exhibitions.

Fountain in the Second Courtyard

Returning to the Second Courtyard [C], you will find the entrance to the **Castle Gallery [U]**. Since 1964 the former stables have housed the remains of the valuable art collections assembled by the Habsburgs during the 16th and 17th century in Prague Castle.

From the Second Courtyard, you can now turn right into the Castle Gardens [V]. Built into a bulwark you will find the entrance to the Spanish Room and the former Rudolf's Gallery, where Rudolf II housed his precious collections of paintings, sculptures, books and jewels. The majority of the items were scattered to the winds during the 17th and 18th century.

At the end of the tour of the Castle Hill proper, it is recommended that you visit the park on the south slope with its Paradise Garden and the Embankment Garden, as well as the Belvedere Summer Palace to the northeast (*see Plan, page 19*). In the Third Courtyard [E] you will find the descent to the **Paradise Garden [W]** (daily except Monday 10am–5.45pm). This charming park originally dates from 1562, but was redesigned in 1920–3 in accordance with plans drawn up by Josip Plečnik.

The circular structure adorning the gardens dates from 1614 when it was built for Emperor Matthias. The attractive weathervane on the roof displays the monogram of the ruler and his wife Anna. Inside the building it is still possible to see the original ceiling paintings, showing the emblems of all the countries in the Habsburg Empire.

Paradise Garden

The wall paintings were completed much later, in 1848. The statue of the *Good Shepherd* in the garden was created by I. Kalvodas in 1922. A focal point of the park is provided by the huge granite basin weighing 40 tonnes.

Immediately adjoining the Paradise Garden is the **Embankment Garden [X]**. The park was laid out in 1928 (also designed by Josip Plečnik) on the site of the castle fortifications, which had been filled in towards the end of the 19th century.

Two baroque obelisks beneath the Ludwig Wing mark the spot where the two imperial governors, Martinicz and Slavata and their secretary (*see page 9*), were thrown from the castle window to the ground. This incident, known as the Second Defenestration of Prague, sparked off the Thirty Years' War.

The two spacious gardens are very popular with the citizens of Prague as a favourite destination for strolling. There are magnificent views of the city and the parks offer an excellent impression of the south facade of the castle, below which they are situated.

To the northeast of the castle, separated from the latter by the Deer Moat, lies the **Belvedere [Z]**, the Pleasure Palace of Queen Anne (Letohrádek královny Anny), wife of Ferdinand I, the first Habsburg emperor (1526–64). It is reached by leaving the castle by the North Gate and crossing the Prašny most bridge (*see page 16*). Passing the former Riding School on your left and the former Royal Gardens on your right, you will arrive at what is considered to be the most important Renaissance building on Bohemian soil. The palace was built between 1538–63 and is the work of several architects, including (from 1538) Giovanni Spatio and (from 1557) Bonifaz Wohlmuth. The copper roof, whose shape recalls an upturned boat, was completed in 1560. The ground plan of the palace is modelled on that of the Temple of Poseidon at Paestum.

In the lovely Renaissance Royal Garden, laid out by Ferdinand I in 1534 and redesigned in 1955, stands the **Ball House [ZA]** (Mičnova), designed by Bonifaz Wohlmuth in 1563–8. It is covered in lovely *sgraffito* work. The famous **Singing Fountain** (Zvivajici fontána **[ZB]**, designed in 1562 by the Italian sculptor Francesco Terzio, also graces the garden. It was cast in 1564 in Bohemia by the bell-founder Tomáš Jaroš and dedicated during the same year in the presence of Emperor Maximilian II. The fountain shows a variety of sculptured details, including flower and animal motifs, Greek gods and – a remarkable curiosity – a bagpipe player.

The Singing Fountain may indeed derive its name in part from this musician, but it is more often attributed to the fact that the drops of water landing in the bronze basin cause it to resound.

The Deer Moat **33**

Route 2

★★★ Prague Castle – Schwarzenberg Palace – Archbishop's Palace – ★★ National Gallery – Tuscany Palace – ★★ Loreto Church – ★★ Strahov Monastery

This route covers three of the city's most important sights: the National Gallery, the Loreto Church and the former Strahov Monastery. *Please refer to the map on page 16.*

On Hradčany Square (Hradčanské náměsti), in front of **Prague Castle ❶** , stand three large palaces: the Schwarzenberg Palace to the south, the Tuscany Palace to the west and the Archbishop's Palace to the north.

The **Schwarzenberg Palace ❷** was originally built in 1543 by Augustin Vlach for the Lobkowitz family, and was acquired by the Schwarzenberg family in 1714. It is one of the loveliest Renaissance buildings in Bohemia; of particular interest are the *sgraffito* paintings on the facades, the rectangular stones of which – in the style of Italian models – have been worked to look like diamonds, as well as the main courtyard and the ceiling frescoes on the second floor.

Today the palace houses a remarkable collection of the Museum of Military History (April to November daily except Monday 10am–6pm).

Archbishop's palace

Opposite lies the **Archbishop's Palace ❸**, built in 1550 and rebuilt several times in 1562–4, 1669–94, 1722–5 and 1764. Its present appearance dates from the last renovations, carried out during the reign of Maria Theresa.

Passing through the left gateway of the palace and taking a passage leading downhill, you will come to the **Sternberg Palace** (1700). Since 1950 it has contained the most important section of the ★★ **National Gallery ❹** (daily except Monday 10am–6pm).

Schwarzenberg Palace

First floor
Displayed in the rooms on the first floor are works by a variety of Italian and Dutch artists of the 14th and 15th century: Archangelo di Cola; Jacopo and Nardo Cione; Lorenzo Monaco; Antonio Vivarna (*Retable with Twelve Saints*); Giovanni d'Alamagna (*The Nativity of Christ*); Piero della Francesca (*Christ with the Saints*); Jan Gossaert, known as Mabuse (*St Luke Painting the Madonna*); Pieter Brueghel the Elder (*The Haymaking*); and Pieter Brueghel the Younger (*The Arrival of the Magi* and *Winter Landscape*).

Lamenting Christ by Lorenzo Monaco

Second floor
Italian painting: a five-panel altarpiece by Orcagna; *Madonna* by Benozzo Gozzoli; *The Madonna with the Veil* by Sebastiano del Piombo; *Madonna with Saints* by Palma il Vecchio; *David with Goliath's Head* and *St Jerome* by Tintoretto; *Summer* and *The Annunciation to the Shepherds* by Bassano the Younger; *Portrait of a Venetian Nobleman* by Tiepolo; *Seascape* by Guardi and *View of London* by Canaletto.

35

German painting: *Madonna Enthroned* (1434) by Hans von Tübingen; *The Beheading of St Barbara* (c 1470) by Hans Schüchlin; the *Hohenburg Altar* (1509) by Hans Holbein the Elder; the *Martyrdom of St Dorothea* (1516) by Hans Baldung Grien; the *Martyrdom of St Florian* (c 1520) by Albrecht Altdorfer; a fragment of an *Altarpiece* (c 1520) by Lucas Cranach the Elder; and – most famous of all – the *Festival of the Rosary* (1506) by Albrecht Dürer.

Festival of the Rosary by Dürer

Dutch painting: triptych depicting the *Adoration of the Magi* by Geertgen tot Sint Jans; *The Fountain of Life* (1511) by the Master of the Fountain of Life; *Abraham and Isaac* by Antony van Dyck; *St Augustine*, the *Martyrdom of St Thomas* and other works by Rubens; the *Portrait of Judge Jasper Schade van Westrum of Utrecht* by Frans Hals; *The Old Scholar* and a fragment of an *Annunciation* by Rembrandt; the *Dance in a Peasant's Room* by Adriaen van Ostade; the *Serenade* by Jan Steen; *Young Lady on a Balcony* by Gerhard Dou; and two paintings by Gerard Terborch.

European painting of the 19th and 20th century: the collection includes works by the Austrian artists Oskar Kokoschka, Gustav Klimt and Egon Schiele; the German artist Max Liebermann and the Norwegian Edvard Munch.

Ground floor
This section contains an excellent collection of 19th- and 20th-century French art.

Of particular interest are: seven paintings by Eugène Delacroix; *The Family on the Barricade* by Honoré Daumier; a number of sculptures (including *The Age of Brass*, *Female Nude* and plaster casts for the Balzac memorial) by Auguste Rodin; two paintings by Jean-Baptiste Corot; *The Bridge at Meudon* by Théodore Rousseau; *Forest Scene*, *Landscape in the Jura* and *The Funeral in Ornans* by Gustave Courbet; *Two Women in a Garden* by Claude Monet; *The Bridge at Sèvres* by Alfred Sisley; three paintings by Camille Pissarro; *The Lovers* by Auguste Renoir; *The Harbour at Honfleur* by Georges Seurat; *The Seine near Samois* by Paul Signac; *Self-Portrait* by Henri Rousseau; three paintings each by Paul Cézanne and Paul Gauguin; *The Green Cornfield* by Vincent van Gogh; *Moulin Rouge* by Toulouse-Lautrec; *Pomona* by Aristide Maillol; *A Conversation in Provence* by Pierre Bonnard; *Joaquina* by Henri Matisse; *Street in the Suburbs* by Maurice Utrillo; *Still Life* by Raoul Dufy; *The Grand Arabesque* by Edgar Degas; five paintings by André Derain; five still life works by Georges Braque; *The Circus* by Marc Chagall and no fewer than 14 works by Pablo Picasso.

Before leaving the gallery you should take a brief look at the garden, where sculptures including *John the Baptist* and *Meditation* by Auguste Rodin are on display.

Leaving the National Gallery, the route continues past the Virgin's Column, created in 1720 by Ferdinand Maximilian Brokoff, to the far end of Hradčany Square, to the **Tuscany Palace ⑤**, believed to have been built in 1695 by Jean-Baptiste Mathey, the French architect whose work dominated Prague at the time. He was also responsible for the Church of the Crusader Knights (*see page 59*) and Troja Palace (*see page 69*).

Skirting to the left of the palace, you will come to the Loreto Square (Loretánské náměstí). Stretched out along the west side is the massive silhouette of the **Czernín Palace** (not open to the public), which today houses the Foreign Ministry. Construction of this monumental building began at the end of the 1660s and continued over half a century. The palace, with its huge Corinthian columns, is a direct result of the fascination which the *palazzi* of the Italian aristocracy held for Jan Humprecht Czernín, the Imperial ambassador to Venice.

The architects commissioned to build the massive palace were for the most part famous Italian masters. The plans were drawn up by Francesco Caratti; their execution was entrusted to Giovanni Capuli, Giovanni Battista Maderna and Egidio Rossi, among others.

After the palace had been partially destroyed by French troops in 1742, it was rebuilt and extended in 1747 by another architect, Anselmo Lurago.

At the beginning of the 19th century the complex was used merely as a military barracks, but in 1928–32 it was

Still life by Georges Braque

The Tuscany Palace

The Czernín Palace

restored once more, the work this time directed by a Bohemian architect, Pavel Janák.

Opposite the Czernín Palace stands the **★★ Loreto
Church ❻** (Tuesday to Sunday 9am–12.15pm and 1–
4.30pm), dedicated to the Virgin Mary and the most famous pilgrimage church in Prague. Building commenced
soon after the victory of the Imperial Catholic armies in
the Battle of the White Mountain (1620). The church's
present-day appearance dates mostly from the first third
of the 18th century.

The Loreto Church

The magnificent baroque facade was completed in
1721–5 and was the work of Christoph Dientzenhofer and
his son Kilian Ignaz. The latter was also responsible for
the forecourt adorned with angels in front of the entrance.
In the tower hangs a glockenspiel of 27 bells, donated in
1694. The total weight of the bells is 1,500kg (1.5 tonnes);
every hour, they play a Czech hymn to the Virgin Mary.

Loreto Church forecourt

The courtyard of the church is surrounded by a two-
storey cloister (1634–1747). In the middle stands a copy
of the famous **Casa Santa** by Bramante, sculpted in
1626–31 by Giovanni Orsi. The original is in Loreto, in
the Italian province of Ancona. According to the legend,
angels supposedly brought the house of the Holy Family from Nazareth via Fiume to Loreto during the 13th century. The windowless, twilit interior was decorated in 1795
with a cycle of frescoes.

Beside the Casa Santa stand two baroque fountains
(1739–40) by Johann Michael Brüderle: on the left, *The
Resurrection of Christ* and on the right, *The Assumption
of the Virgin Mary* (a replica). The 45 arches of the lower
cloister were painted by Felix Anton Scheffler in 1750
with symbols from the *Litany of the Blessed Virgin*, a
prayer of incantation. The six chapels house a number
of remarkable works of art.

In the middle of the east wing, previously also the site
of a chapel, now stands the **Church of the Nativity**, begun in 1717 by Christoph Dientzenhofer, continued by his
son and finished by his stepson Georg Achbauer in 1734.

Church of the Nativity, interior

The purity of style and harmonious balance of the interior of the church make it one of the most charming examples of Prague baroque art. A multitude of angels and
cherubs, prophets, apostles and saints seem to fill the space
with life as if on a stage. The skilful use of light makes
some figures and groups gleam more brightly than others.
Of particular interest are the exquisitely decorated organ
(1734–8) and the three ceiling paintings: the *Presentation
in the Temple* (1735–6) by Wenzel Lorenz Reiner beside
the high altar, the *Adoration of the Shepherds* and the *Adoration of the Magi* (1742) by Johann Adam Schöpf.

Finally, a visit to the Treasury is well worthwhile,
housed since 1962 on the first floor of the entrance wing.

Diamond Monstrance

It houses approximately 300 items of widely varying artistic merit. The masterpiece of the whole collection is the famous ★★ **Diamond Monstrance**, manufactured in Vienna in 1699 by a goldsmith named Künischbauer, and Stegner, a jeweller, possibly to a design by Johann Bernhard Fischer von Erlach. The monstrance weighs 12kg (26.4lbs) and is of gilded silver encrusted with 6,222 diamonds. Also worthy of note are the six other monstrances dating from 1673–1740; two are gold, and the remainder of gilded silver. The collection also includes a Gothic chalice dating from 1510, a pacifical decorated with rock crystals and garnets dating from 1631, a home altar of ivory and silver (c 1600), crucifixes and mitres.

From the Loreto Square turn right by the Czernín Palace to the Pohořelec (Place of the Fire), which at this point opens up to form a square. Take a small arched staircase at house No 8 (or the main entrance, a little further to the west) which leads to the former ★★ **Strahov Monastery** ➐, one of the most famous and most visited sights in the city (Tuesday to Sunday 9am–12 noon and 1–5pm).

Strahov Monastery Church

The Monastery of the Premonstratensians was founded in 1148 by Vladislav I, the King of Bohemia at the time. During the 16th–17th century the complex was rebuilt, acquiring its present appearance at the end of the 18th century. Since 1950 it has been completely restored; in 1953 it became the Museum of National Literature.

On the right is the library building; if you go up to the first floor, you will find the magnificent baroque rooms of the former monastery library.

You will enter first of all the two-storey ★ **Philosophers' Library**, built in 1782–4 by Ignaz Palliardi, which measures 32m (102ft) long by 10m (32ft) wide and 14m (45ft) high. The main attraction, apart from the baroque bookcases, is the remarkable ceiling fresco, completed in 1794 in a period of only six months by Franz Anton Maulpertsch, Austria's most famous rococo artist, who was 70 years of age when he did the work together with his assistant Marin Michl.

Four great eras of mankind are depicted here with a large number of identifiable individual figures. As you enter, along the length of the room are the Mythological Age (left) and the Age of Ancient Greece (left and right); on the short side opposite the entrance is the Christian Era. The end of the cycle above the central section on the right-hand side is represented by the Triumph of Heavenly Wisdom at the end of the world.

The corridor linking the library to the second room houses medical, legal and scientific books; in a glass display case is a facsimile of the famous *Strahov Gospel*, thought to have been written in about 800 in Trier. The four excellent portraits of the evangelists were added later, and date from about 900. The magnificent binding dates from the 12th–17th centuries.

At the end of the corridor are steps leading down into the Theological Library, which is closed for renovation at present. It was constructed in 1671–9 by Giovanni Domenico Orsi and extended by two arches in 1721. The ceiling frescoes were painted in 1723–7 by Siard Nosecký, a member of the monastery. Apart from the theological books, the room also houses 17th-century globes and glass cases displaying magnificent manuscripts.

Back on the ground floor, the former cloister and the adjoining rooms (access only from outside, past the monastery church) house the ★ **Museum of National Literature** (Památník národniho písemnictvi; Tuesday to Sunday 9am–12.15pm and 1–5pm). The collection provides a comprehensive survey of the history of Czech literature from the 9th century to the present day, with a particular emphasis on the pre-Hussite and Hussite eras. No other European people possesses such a complete, clearly presented account of its literary history. The collection comprises some 130,000 volumes, including 3,000 manuscripts and 2,500 first editions. Due to lack of space, only a small proportion of the collection can be displayed at any one time.

Museum of National Literature

39

Among the exhibited manuscripts, of particular importance are the 9th-century Strahov Gospel – not only the oldest manuscript in the library, but one of the oldest first editions of a Coptic manuscript; and a first-edition copy of Copernicus' work *De revolutionibus orbium coelestium* ('On the revolutions of the celestial orbs'). In this series of six volumes, Copernicus published his heliocentric theory of the structure of the universe.

On leaving the museum it is worth taking the passage opposite as it affords a fine view of Hradčany.

From the monastery courtyard, turn left towards the main gate mentioned on page 38. On the left stands the former monastery Church of Our Lady (not open to the public at present), which developed from a Romanesque basilica and acquired its present appearance during the 17th–18th century. The interior, which is richly adorned in the baroque style, contains the tomb of the commander of the Imperial army, General Count Pappenheim, who died in the Battle of Lützen (1632). In 1787, Mozart played on the baroque organ, which dates from 1740.

The Library Building standing near the monastery church was built in 1782–4 by the Italian architect Palliardi in a style which marks the transition from late baroque to classicism. But the little Chapel of St Rochus near the main entrance is still predominantly Gothic in style, although it was built in 1603–11. It is used today as an exhibition hall.

View of Hradčany

St Nicholas' Church,
Malá Strana

Route 3

★★ The Lesser Quarter (Malá Strana): Malostranské náměsti – Waldstein Palace – Church of St Mary in Chains – Kampa Island

A break for budding talent

Lesser Quarter Square

Extending from below Hradčany down to the Vltava, the Malá Strana is one of the oldest and most interesting parts of the city. After the Battle of the White Mountain (1620) it became the favoured residential area of the aristocracy which had remained loyal to the emperor; this explains why the district contains a large number of fine patrician mansions. *For this route please refer to the map of central Prague on pages 12–13.*

From Castle Hill the Lesser Quarter and its focal point, the Lesser Quarter Square (Malostranské náměstí), can be reached via the Nové zámecké schody or by taking the Nerudova ul. (*see page 42*). You will also come to the Malostranské náměsti by taking two right turns on the way downhill, traversing the Valdštejnská and passing the Waldstein Palace (*see page 42*). The Malostranské náměsti can also be reached directly via the Charles Bridge (*see page 45*) by taking the Mostecká ul.

Malostranské náměsti (Lesser Quarter Square), the large, enclosed square at the heart of the Lesser Quarter, evolved during the 13th century, but was completely remodelled during the baroque era (17th–18th centuries). Since then it has been divided into two separate squares by the massive complex of St Nicholas' Church and the former Jesuit College; the modern name, Malostranské náměstí, applies to both but was not adopted until 1869.

At the end of the 18th century the House of the Stone Table was built onto the end of the choir of St Nicholas' Church; today it houses the Lesser Quarter Café (Malostranské kavárna), which was a popular rendezvous for Prague and émigré German artists between the wars.

On the north and east sides of the square are a number of elegant facades dating from the baroque and rococo eras, in some cases later additions to medieval buildings. Thus the Lesser Quarter Town Hall (No 22) dates from 1479, and No 23 combines three narrow old houses dating from the 14th century – as does the house U Montágů (No 18) on the north side.

The focal point of the square is **St Nicholas' Church** (Chrám sv. Mikuláše) ❽, the largest and most impressive baroque church in Prague. On the site of a Gothic church which had been dedicated in 1283 and demolished during the 17th century, Christoph Dientzenhofer built the nave and the facade in 1703–17; his son, Kilian Ignaz Dientzenhofer, added the choir, the dome and the tower in 1737–52. The tower was then completed by Anselmo Lurago in 1755. The church adjoins the Collegiate Building which was erected for the Jesuits in 1673–90 by Domenico Orsi de Orsini.

St Nicholas' Church

The west front of the church is divided into three sections and surmounted by a gable; it is decorated with statues of the patron saint, St Peter the Apostle and St Paul, as well as the founding saints of the Jesuit order, Ignatius Francisco Xavier, and the Fathers of the Church, Saints Ambrosius, Gregory, Jerome and Augustine.

Today the interior is dominated by the vast choir added by Kilian Ignaz Dientzenhofer to the nave designed by his father. The observation tower on the Petřín Hill would fit inside the vast dome, which is 75m (240ft) high and is supported by four slanting pillars. The dome fresco, the *Glorification of the Holy Trinity*, was painted by Franz Xaver Palko in 1752–3. The figures on the pillars of the intersection, the work of Ignaz Platzer (1769), represent four eastern teachers of the church.

Interior of St Nicholas

The main attraction inside the church is without doubt the vast ceiling fresco, painted by the Viennese artist Johann Lukas Kracker in 1760–1. It covers an area of 1,500sq m (16,150sq ft) and depicts the *Apotheosis of St Nicholas*. The saint, who was Bishop of Myra in Asia Minor at the beginning of the 4th century, is honoured as the preserver of justice and the patron saint of town administrations, merchants and seafarers. The fresco shows the saint in the middle, surrounded by angels. Below is a triumphal arch with the saint's tomb; on the right can be seen the liberation of three Roman officers who had been sentenced to death, and on the left is a mythical landscape with merchants and sailors.

The dome fresco

On the square in front of the church, also known as the Upper Square, stands a Trinity Column dating from 1715. Opposite is the Lichtenstein Palace (1791). Here begins the Nerudova ulice, formerly known as Spur Alley. Today it is the principal approach road to the district of Hradčany (*see page 40*).

(*see page 40*)

The street, bordered by fine townhouses and mansions, has largely retained its historic appearance characteristic of the Prague high baroque era. In accordance with ancient custom, most of the houses bear names and painted signs: The Three Violins (No 12), St John Nepomuk (No 18), The Golden Horseshoe (No 33), The Black Madonna (No 36) and The Two Suns (No 47), the home of the Czech writer Jan Neruda (1834–91), the author of *Tales of the Lesser Quarter*.

The Two Suns

The row of houses is interrupted by two magnificent baroque palaces: the Thun-Hohenstein Palace (No 20 – today the Italian Embassy), erected in 1710–20 by Johann Blasius Santini-Aichel as the Kolowrat Palace – and the Czernin-Morzin Palace, the work of the same architect, built in 1713–14 and today the Romanian Embassy.

It is worth making another detour from the Malostranské náměstí, this time in a northerly direction, to walk along the Tomášská past the house The Golden Stag (No 4), with the prettiest painted house sign in the city, to Waldstein Square (Valdštejnské náměstí).

Waldstein Palace

The right-hand side of the square is occupied by the **Waldstein Palace** ❾, the first major secular baroque building in Prague. After the Battle of the White Mountain in 1620, the general of the imperial army, Albrecht von Wallenstein, whose real name was Waldstein, purchased and demolished 23 houses on this site. On the land thus cleared he commissioned Italian architects to build the vast palace in 1623–30. The lovely interior, including Wallenstein's circular study, a two-storey banqueting hall and the private chapel, are not open to the public at the time of going to press, due to renovation work.

Sculpture in the Palace Gardens

Well worth visiting are the **Palace Gardens** (May to September 9am–7pm); the entrance can be reached via the Letenská. Opening onto the garden is a magnificent loggia, known as the Sala Terrena, where concerts are sometimes held during the spring and summer months.

A number of fine sculptures will be found in the garden. The originals were the work of Adriaen de Vries in 1622–6, but in 1648 they were captured as booty by Swedish soldiers, during the Thirty Years' War, and taken to Drottningholm. In 1914–15 they were replaced by good copies. Beginning at the Sala Terrena, there is a horse on the left, followed by Venus and Adonis, Neptune and Apollo. To the right is a second horse, then a group of wrestlers, Laokoon and Bacchus.

42

Crossing the park or walking along Waldstein Alley you will come to the former **Waldstein Riding School** . The fine building today houses changing exhibitions.

The Waldstein Riding School

43

Waldstein Alley (Valdštejnská) begins at Waldstein Square. On the left stand a number of lovely mansions dating from the 18th century: the Ledebur Palace, rebuilt during the 19th century (No 3) with a charming terrace garden and a lovely Sala Terrena dating from 1716; the Kolowrat Palace (No 10) with a facade dating from 1784; and the Fürstenberg Palace (No 14), built in 1743–7.

Returning along Tomašská Street, turn left at the Lesser Quarter Square, following the tram lines, into the Josefka Street. On the left is the **Church of St Thomas** (Kostel sv. Tomáše) . Founded in 1285 by Wenceslas II, the original Early Gothic building was reconstructed in the baroque style in 1725 by Kilian Ignaz Dientzenhofer, after it had been struck by lightening.

Tram approaching the square

Continuing right along Josefka Street, the Carmelite Church of St Joseph (1673–92) is situated on the left-hand side. Josefka leads to Bridge Street (Mostecká), with the Kaunitz Palace (No 15), a lovely mansion with a rococo facade, built in 1773 by Anton Schmidt.

A left turn into the Mostecká, which links the Lesser Quarter Square with the Charles Bridge, followed by a right turn into Lázeňská Street, leads to the former Church of the Knights of Malta, the **Church of St Mary in Chains** (Kostel Panny Marie pod řetězem)  (the chains were used in the Middle Ages to close the gatehouse of the knights' monastery). The original 12th-century building was demolished and later building work was left unfinished. Only the choir was completed and now serves – sep-

Golden Unicorn

Boating fun on Kampa Island

Strolling on Petřín Hill

arated from the main facade by the two 14th-century towers – as a church. It was renovated in around 1640 and its main points of interest are the magnificent altars.

Diagonally opposite stand the former Wolkenstein Palace (No 11) and the famous tavern **The Golden Unicorn**, in which Beethoven stayed while visiting the city in 1796. To the left is the Great Priory Square (Velkopřevorské náměstí), with the baroque Great Priory Palace (No 4), built in 1726–38, the adjoining Garden of the Knights of Malta and the Buquoy-Longueval Palace (No 2), dating from 1682 and rebuilt in 1738. The latter now houses the French Embassy.

Creating an extension of the square is a small bridge leading to **Kampa Island** (Ostrov Kampa), formed by a narrow branch of the Vltava, the **Devil's Canal** (Čertovka). It is pleasant to take a short walk through its pretty gardens and past the old houses to the Lichtenstein Palace (1696). There is a magnificent view of the Charles Bridge and the Old and New Towns.

After this detour return to Great Priory Square and the Church of St Mary in Chains, bearing left from there towards the Square of the Knights of Malta (Maltézské náměstí). Of particular note are the Statue of St John (1715) by Ferdinand Maximilian Brokoff, erected in thanks for the end of an epidemic of plague; the Old Post (No 8) and – at the south end of the square – the former Nostitz Palace, built in 1658–60. In 1720 the facade was redesigned in the baroque style before acquiring its rococo features in 1770. Part of the building is now home to the Dutch Embassy.

From the Maltézské náměstí the Harantova leads back to the Karmelitská, the main thoroughfare of the Lesser Quarter. Bearing to the left, there is another detour to Petřín Hill (*see page 67*), from where there is a magnificent view of Prague. Bearing right back towards the Lesser Quarter Square, however, leads to the **Church of Our Lady of Victory** (Chrám Panny Marie Vitězné) ⓭, the city's earliest baroque place of worship (1611–13). Originally a Lutheran church, it was given to the Carmelites in 1624, who re-dedicated it to Our Lady of Victory (after the Battle of the White Mountain).

Inside the church, known for its fine altars, is the highly revered statue of the Infant Jesus of Prague, preserved here since 1628 on the central side altar on the left. The wax figure, some 60cm (23in) high, is of Spanish origin and is famous for the miraculous powers it is said to possess. It is always dressed in precious garments.

It is also well worth visiting the baroque terraced garden (c 1720) of the **Vrtba Palace** (Karmelitska 25), which has fine views of the castle and the Lesser Quarter, and classical statues by Matthias Braun.

Route 4

The ★★ Charles Bridge

One of Prague's loveliest and most characteristic sights, the Charles Bridge connects the Lesser Quarter with the Old Town. It also combines in unique fashion the original Gothic architecture with baroque sculpture.

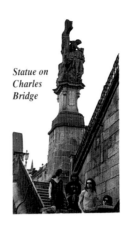

Statue on Charles Bridge

The first stone bridge was constructed here during the second half of the 12th century in the place of a 10th-century wooden bridge which was situated somewhat further to the north. Known as the Judith Bridge after the consort of King Vladislav I, it still exists today in the pillar foundations in the Vltava and the smaller of the bridge towers on the Lesser Quarter side.

In 1342 the Judith Bridge collapsed. In 1357, Charles IV laid the foundation stone for the new, Gothic, construction. Building began under the supervision of the cathedral architect, Peter Parler, who was only 27 at the time. However, the bridge was not completed until 1399, after Parler's death.

Parler's last work was the magnificent **Old Town Bridge Tower** ⓮ (*see map, page 12*), which marks the entrance to the bridge. This vast construction, standing on the first bridge support, is decorated with fine sculptures on its east side. High up, in a gallery of tracery, stand St Adalbert (left), the second bishop of Prague, and St Wenceslas (right). Below, in a rounded arch, is Charles IV (left); on a foreshortened representation of the Charles Bridge is St Vitus (centre) and finally Wenceslas IV (right). Further down again is a row with the coats of arms of the Holy Roman Empire (inside left), Bohemia (inside right) and the Luxembourg domains. Here – and elsewhere on the tower – is Wenceslas IV's personal emblem: a kingfisher in a 'love knot', a knotted handkerchief. Equally elaborate sculptures on the bridge side of the tower were destroyed in 1648 during the Swedish occupation. A memorial plaque recalls the Thirty Years' War.

45

Slightly curved, the **Charles Bridge** (*Karlův most*) ⓯ is 510m (558 yards) long and 10m (32ft) wide. It spans the Vltava by means of 17 pillars, strengthened on both sides and forming 16 arches. It is one of Prague's main tourist thoroughfares, particularly in the summertime when artists set up their stalls and buskers entertain the throngs.

Charles Bridge

During the Middle Ages the bridge had no sculptural decoration, relying for effect on its harmonious proportions and massive arches made of carefully worked stones, as well as on the towers at each end. The only adornment in those days was a *Crucifix* (5), subsequently renewed on several occasions.

The 30 statues adorning the bridge were added over a period of 250 years. Nonetheless, visually they form a har-

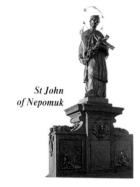

**St John
of Nepomuk**

The Crucifixion group

Statue of St Wenceslas

monious whole in spite of their widely varying artistic merits. Many of them are copies. The originals are now kept in the Lapidarium of the National Museum in the Stromovka Park.

The first statue to be added to the bridge was that of St John of Nepomuk (15), which was placed near the point where John, the Vicar General and deputy bishop, who was canonised in 1729, was thrown into the Vltava and drowned in 1393 on the orders of Wenceslas IV. Between 1706–14, 21 further statues were erected on the bridge. The most important baroque sculptors whose work can be seen here are Johann Brokoff (15), his son Ferdinand Maximilian Brokoff (15) (4, 10, 14, 20, 23, 27, 28) and the Tyrolean artist Matthias Bernhard Braun (2, 16, 24).

1 *The Virgin Mary with St Bernhard* (1709) by Matthias Wenzel Jäckel (replica).
2 *St Ivo* (1711; replica made in 1928) by Matthias Bernhard Braun.
3 *The Virgin with Ss Dominic and Thomas Aquinas* (1708; replica made in 1961) by Matthias Wenzel Jäckel.
4 *Ss Barbara, Margaret and Elizabeth* (1707) by Ferdinand Maximilian Brokoff
5 Crucifixion group with a crucifix dating from 1629 and figures from 1861.
6 *Pietà* (1859) by Emanuel Max.
7 *St Anne with the Virgin Mary and Infant Jesus* (1707) by Matthias Wenzel Jäckel.
8 *St Joseph* (1854) by Emanuel Max.
9 *Ss Cyril and Methodius* (1928) by Karel Dvořák.
10 *St Francis Xavier* (1711; copy dating from 1913) by Ferdinand Maximilian Brokoff.
11 *St John the Baptist* (1857) by Josef Max.
12 *St Christopher* (1857) by Emanuel Max.
13 *Ss Wenceslas, Norbert and Sigismund* (1853) by Josef Max.
14 *St Francis Borgia* (1710) by Ferdinand Maximilian Brokoff.
15 *St John of Nepomuk* (1683); model by Johann Brokoff, reliefs by Matthias Rauchmüller, cast by W. Heroldt.16 *St Ludmilla* (c 1720) from the atelier of Matthias Bernhard Braun.

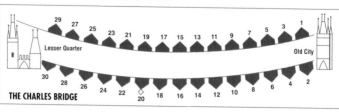

THE CHARLES BRIDGE

17 *St Anthony of Padua* (1707) by Johann Meyer.

18 *St Francis the Seraphic* (1855) by Emanuel Max.

19 *St Judas Thaddeus* (1708) by Johann Meyer.

20 *Ss Vincent of Ferrer and Procop* (1712) by Ferdinand Maximilian Brokoff. To the left, beneath the bridge, stands a late Gothic column with a statue of Roland (copy, 1884). The legendary hero of the *Song of Roland*, known in Czech as Brunsvík (i.e. the Knight of Brunswick), who won the friendship of a lioness, is the patron of the bridge.

21 *St Augustine* (1708) by Johann Friedrich Kohl (copy).

22 *St Nicholas of Tolentino* (1708) by Johann Friedrich Kohl (copy).

23 *St Cajetan* (1709) by Ferdinand Maximilian Brokoff.

24 *St Luitgard* (1710) by Matthias Bernhard Braun (considered to be the sculpture with the greatest artistic merit and made when Braun was only 26).

25 *St Philip Benitius* (1714) by Michael Bernhard Mandl (copy).

26 *St Adalbert* (1709) by Joseph Michael Brokoff (copy).

27 *St Vitus* (1714) by Ferdinand Maximilian Brokoff.

28 *Ss John of Matha, Felix of Valois and Ivan* (1714) by Ferdinand Maximilian Brokoff (the figure of the Turk is particularly well-loved).

29 *Ss Cosmas and Damian* (1709) by Johann Meyer.

30 *St Wenceslas* (1858) by Joseph Kamill Böhm.

47

A place for contemplation

Lesser Quarter Bridge Tower ⑯: the tower on the left (south) side is a relic from the Judith Bridge (1158–72; *see page 45*). The right-hand (north) tower was erected later, in 1464.

Lesser Quarter Bridge Tower

Route 5

From ★★ Wenceslas Square to the Old Town Square
– ★ Estates Theatre – Carolinum – Old Town Hall –
★★ Old Town Square – Teyn Church – Church of St
James – Church of St Nicholas

The Charles Bridge marks the beginning of the Old Town
(Staré město), which can conveniently be visited following the tour of Hradčany and the Lesser Quarter. It is recommended, however, that at least one day be reserved
for the visit to the Old Town. It is thus more practical to
begin the tour at ★★ Wenceslas Square, in the vicinity of
which will be found most of the hotels. *Please refer to
the map on pages 12–13.*

From Wenceslas Square (*see page 61*), take the narrow alley Na můstku at the far end, which leads into the
Old Town. Before continuing straight ahead towards the
Old Town Square, however, make a short detour by turning right into the Rytířská ulice, at the end of which stands
the ★ Estates Theatre (Stavovské divadlo) **17**. Renovated
in 1990–1, this theatre was actually the first in the city.
Built in 1781–3, it was inaugurated as the Nostitz Theatre on 21 April 1783 with a performance of Lessing's
Emilia Galotti. On 29 October 1787 it was also the setting
for the first performance of Mozart's *Don Giovanni*, which
he had completed in Prague. From 1798 it was known as
the Estates Theatre, and from the middle of the 19th century as the German National Theatre. After World War
II it was named after the playwright and actor Josef Ka-
jetán (1808–56), who worked here as a dramatist. It was
during one of his comedies that today's Czech national an-
them was heard for the first time. Today, plays and operas are performed here.

Immediately on the left stands the **Carolinum 18**, the
original building of the university founded in Prague by
Charles IV in 1348 and thus the oldest university in Central Europe.

The building was based on a house constructed in about
1370 on this very site; all that remains today is a
magnificent Gothic oriel window designed by the school
of Peter Parler. The baroque facade dates from 1718 and
was rebuilt in the neo-Gothic style; between 1934–50 it
was restored in a way which was largely faithful to its original Gothic appearance.

From here you can continue directly to the Old Town
Square, but a small detour is recommended. First bear left
and follow the Havelská ulice to the Church of St Gal-
lus (sv. Havel), originally Gothic but now furnished with
a fine baroque facade (1690–1700), then turn right into
Melantrichova Street. On the corner of Kožná ulička stands

The Estates Theatre

Oriel window, Carolinum

Taking it in their stride

the house called To the Two Bears (c 1570), in which the 'roving reporter' Egon Erwin Kisch was born in 1885 and subsequently lived for many years.

The Two Bears

Melantrichova Street ends opposite the **Old Town Hall** (Staroměstská radnice) ⑲ (Tuesday to Saturday 9am–5pm, with a conducted tour every hour on the hour). Its history stretches back as far as 1338, when King John of Luxembourg permitted the citizens of the 'old town of Prague' (in contrast to the 'Lesser Quarter') to convert their burghers' assembly hall into a town hall. The tower was added in 1364, followed in 1381 by the Gothic oriel chapel. The Late Gothic portal was built in about 1460; to the right stands the famous astronomical clock, built in 1410 (see below). During the first half of the 16th century, a Renaissance-style extension was added to the left which boasts a fine triple window group and the inscription *Praga Caput Regni*. To the left of that, the adjoining building dates from 1897.

The ★★ **Astronomical Clock** consists of a calendar dial (at the bottom), a clock dial (above) and the Procession of Apostles (at the top), which was added during the 19th century. The Calendar Dial moves on one position at midnight every day; the signs of the zodiac and the representations of the months with scenes from rural life were painted by Josef Mánes in 1864–5 (these are replicas).

The Clock Dial marks with Arabic figures round the outside of the face the 24 hours from one sunset to the next; beneath, in Roman numbers, it indicates our modern time divisions. The circle above the dial depicts the signs of the zodiac; a golden pointer indicates the month and the position and phase of the moon and the sun. Finally, twelve arched rays mark the nightly position of the planets.

The Astronomical Clock and Apostles on the Clock

Crowds awaiting the hour

Clowning in the Square

The Kinsky Palace

Every hour, on the hour, to the delight of the waiting tourists assembled below, the two windows above the clock face open to reveal the procession of the twelve apostles; six to the right and six to the left. Then the windows close once more, a cock crows tinnily, and Death turns the hourglass over and rings the death knell.

It is also possible to visit the interior of the Town Hall. From the Entrance Hall (with 19th-century mosaic pictures), the visitor enters the Late Gothic Council Chamber, with a magnificent beamed ceiling, coats of arms and symbols of the handworkers' guilds. A Renaissance portal (1619) leads into the new Assembly Chamber (1879); the two monumental paintings by Václav Brožík depict *Jan Hus before the Council in Constance* and *The Election of George of Podebrady as King of Bohemia*, which took place in 1458 in the Old Town Hall.

Finally, the visitor has the opportunity to enjoy the magnificent panorama from the Town Hall Tower, almost 70m (230ft) high (with a lift from the second floor).

Leaving the Town Hall, you should turn left towards the ★★ **Old Town Square** (Staroměstské náměstí). On three sides it is enclosed by Gothic, Renaissance, baroque and rococo-style buildings, which form a harmonious unity despite the contrasting architectural styles. On the fouth (west) side, a neo-Gothic extension was added to the Town Hall in 1838–48, but it was destroyed during the May Uprising of 1945.

The spacious market square became the city's focal point for gatherings and executions. In 1437, 56 Hussite soldiers were put to death here, and on the order of Ferdinand II, the 27 leaders of the rebellion of 1618 were executed here on 21 June 1621: noblemen and ordinary citizens, Germans and Czechs (24 of them by a single executioner); crosses set in the ground and a plaque on the Town Hall recall the event.

To the north of the square stands the imposing **Monument to Jan Hus**. It was the work of Ladislav Šaloun and was erected on this spot in 1915 to mark the 500th anniversary of the death at the stake of the Czech reformer and religious hero Jan Hus in Constance.

To the right is a fine rococo building jutting out into the square. The former **Kinsky Palace** ㉟, was built in 1755–65 by Anselmo Lurago to a design by Kilian Ignaz Dientzenhofer, who had died before his plans could be realised. During the 19th century the palace housed a German grammar school attended by the writer Franz Kafka. Today the palace contains the excellent Graphics Collection of the National Gallery. Changing exhibitions are also held here (daily except Monday 10am–6pm).

Opposite the Old Town Hall, between Týnská and Celetná, stands the building which once housed the Teyn

School, characterised by Romanesque cellar arches, a Late Gothic arcade and Renaissance gables.

Behind the former Teyn School, and accessible through it, is the **Teyn Church** (Týnský chram) . Its landmark 80-m (256-ft) tower dominates the entire Old Town. The characteristic Teyn gable (1463) is crowned by a gilt Madonna (1626) (Tuesday to Friday 1–4pm; Saturday and Sunday 2–5pm).

Teyn Church towers

The present building was erected between 1365 and 1511 on the site of the little Romanesque church of the Virgin Mary (12th century). There was a long interruption in the building programme during the Hussite Wars. The North Tower, which was destroyed by fire in 1819, was restored to its original form in 1835.

King George of Podebrady (1458–71) had a stone chalice covered with gold foil set into the gable niche between the two towers, as a symbol of the Hussite faith. After the Catholic victory (1620) it was replaced by a statue of the Virgin Mary; the Hussite chalice was melted down to make the crown, halo and sceptre.

The unusually high interior was partly rebuilt in the baroque style following a fire during the 17th century. The first great Bohemian baroque artist, Karel Skréta (1610–74), painted the High Altar picture of *The Assumption of the Virgin Mary* and four side altars. The baroque vaulting was added in 1679, when the windows were also altered and the pillars added.

Also of interest are the older works of art, including the Altar of the Cross (1330–40) in the north aisle, a Gothic *Madonna* (c 1400), the pewter Baptismal Font (1414) – the oldest in the city – the Late Gothic Pulpit (15th century), and the Stone Baldaquin (1493) above the grave of the Utraquist bishop Augustinus Lucianus.

By the last pillar on the right-hand side stands the marble tombstone of the Danish astronomer Tycho Brahe (1546–1601), who worked and died in Prague during the reign of Rudolf II. The scholar lost the tip of his nose in a duel or brawl and had to wear a silver prothesis which can be seen on the tombstone. To the right, in the aisle, stands the oldest pewter font in Prague; it dates from 1414.

Leave the church and skirt round the outside to the North Door (in the Týnska ulice), in order to study the magnificent tympanum (c 1400), which depicts scenes from the Passion of Christ (the Scourging, the Crucifixion and the Crown of Thorns). The original sculpture is due to be replaced by a copy.

Passing through a handsome archway (1559–60) you will come to the Teyn. This is one of the oldest market places in the city, with a history stretching back as far as the 10th century. The Granvský House immediately on your left in the courtyard also dates from 1559–60.

If you continue along the Štupartská ulice and the Malá Štupartská ulice, which contains a number of interesting houses: The Eye of God and The Three Paintings (St Wenceslas, Charles IV and George of Podebrady), you will eventually come to the **Church of St James** (*Kostel sv. Jakuba*) **22**. Founded in 1232, the church was rebuilt in 1318–74 and renovated in the baroque style in 1689–1702. Of interest are the unusual reliefs on the facade, carved in 1690–1702 by the Italian sculptor Ottavio Mosta: St Francis (left), St James (centre) and St Anthony (right). It is noticeable that the reliefs are transformed into sculptures in some places, whereas in others they seem to be buried in the wall.

Baroque reliefs, Church of St James

The baroque conversion of the interior was particularly successful. The three rows of arches in the choir, linked to the two-storey nave, are exceptionally fine. The impressive painting on the High Altar, the *Martyrdom of St James*, was painted by Wenzel Lorenz Reiner in 1739. Concerts are often held in the church.

Of note amongst the many other works of art is the magnificent Tomb of Count Vratislav von Mitrowitz (at the end of the aisle). Designed by Johann Bernhard Fischer von Erlach, it was executed in 1714–16 by Ferdinand Maximilian Brokoff. The dying Count is depicted in full battledress. To the right is Chronos, with a beard; to the left, the Angel of Glory, and below on the left stands the allegorical figure of Mourning.

Leave the Church of St James, retrace your steps to the Old Town Square, and cross it diagonally towards the **Church of St Nicholas 23**. Not to be confused with the church of the same name in the Lesser Quarter, and founded in 1272 by German merchants, the Church of St Nicholas was rebuilt in 1732–7 in the baroque style by Kilian Ignaz Dientzenhofer (1689–1751), the supreme master of the Bohemian late baroque style.

Church of St Nicholas, Lesser Quarter

The church had a very chequered history: It once served as a warehouse and in 1870–1914 as a Russian Ortho-

dox church. Since 1920 it has belonged to the Czechoslovak Hussite Church, which was also founded here.

Today the church seems an integral part of the Old Town Square, but until 1901 it was separated from the latter by the Krenn House, which jutted out into the square alongside the Town Hall. The imposing facade was by no means designed with today's long-distance perspective in view, but was planned to be surveyed in close-up. If you approach the facade you will get a good impression of the effect it must have created in times past. The sculptures are the work of Anton Braun, a nephew of the famous Matthias Braun.

Of particular interest, however, is the masterly arrangement of the interior, by means of which Dientzenhofer created an impressive dome section despite the relatively small area which the building occupies. The central area is enclosed by the choir and chapels.

Larger-than-lifesize statues of saints by Anton Braun and frescoes by the Bavarian artist Peter Asam the Elder adorn the cupola. The copious stucco is the work of Bernardo Spinetti. The large metal chandelier with crystal decoration was commissioned by the Russian Orthodox church at the end of the 19th century from the Bohemian glass-blowing factory in Harrachov.

Chandelier in St Nicholas

53

A building standing to the left of the church served as a monastery until 1785. Until the middle of the 19th century it was used as an archive and then as a theatre. (Among other musical works, Mozart's *Don Giovanni* was performed here in 1832.) When the house known as The Tower was rebuilt here on the corner of the Maislova, a doorway from the damaged building was incorporated. As the modern plaque recalls, the writer Franz Kafka was born here on 3 July 1883. The house is now a small museum, devoted to the enigmatic writer.

Plaque on Kafka's house

From here, the Kaprová leads down to the Vltava; the road became famous on account of the novel *The House in the Kaprová*, written by MY Ben-graviel and subsequently filmed. A right turn into the Maislova eventually leads to the former ghetto or Jewish Quarter, but the Kaprová runs down to a broad street called 17 Listopadu (17 November Street), in which the Museum of Industrial Art at No 2 is well worth a visit.

From the north of the Old Town Square, the Pařížská (Paris Street) branches off towards the northwest. Created over a century ago within the framework of an arbitrary restoration programme for the Josefov (*see Route 6*), its magnificent art nouveau facades make it the most spectacular street in the entire city. In the first street on the right, the Salvátorská, stands the Protestant Church of the Redeemer, built in 1611–14 by the Grisons master builder Johann Christoph.

Pařížská

Route 6

Gateway in the Jewish Quarter

Jewish Town Hall: detail

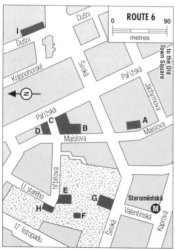

The former ★★ Jewish Quarter

Circled numbers refer to the map on pages 12–13, letters in brackets to the map below.

In the detailed description of Prague dated 965, which we owe to the Jewish merchant Abraham ben Jakob, there is mention of Prague's Jewish community. The ghetto, built in about 1100 and surrounded by a wall, soon became one of the largest Jewish communities in Europe.

Under Ferdinand I (1526–64), there were a number of acts of violence directed against Jews; in 1541 they were banned from the country, and only 15 Jewish families remained in Prague. But under the tolerant emperors Maximilian II (1563–76) and Rudolf II (1576–1612), the ghetto expanded to a total of over 7,000 inhabitants.

After 1848 the ghetto became the fifth district of the provincial capital. It was christened Josefov (Joseph's Town) in honour of Joseph II (1780–90), who had issued the Edict of Tolerance in favour of the Jews. During the 19th century, the sanitary conditions became progressively more intolerable: there were neither water mains nor sanitation, and the number of cases of typhus and cholera rose dramatically. In 1893, a programme of urban development began: block by block, the houses were pulled down and replaced by new buildings in the style of the time. Only six of an original total of 17 synagogues remained intact, plus the Jewish Town Hall and the Old Jewish Cemetery.

Before the German invasion (1939), almost 40,000 Jews lived in Prague; during the course of the war, more than 36,000 of them were murdered by the Nazis in concentration camps.

It was Hitler's intention to establish a major Jewish museum in Prague following his 'Final Victory'. It was to be the museum of an extinct race, and so he issued instructions to the 153 Jewish communities of the Protectorate of Bohemia and Moravia to provide Jewish handicrafts, ritual objects, books and documents, which thus escaped destruction and today form the most valuable collection of its kind in the world.

The collections are displayed in the synagogues which are no longer required for worship. Together with the Ancient Reformed synagogues and the New Jewish Cemetery, all of which are under state protection, they form the **National Museum of Jewish Culture** (Státní muzeum) ㉔ (daily, except Saturday 9am–12 noon and 1–5pm; winter until 4.30pm). The Old New Synagogue closes on Friday at 2pm.

Following Maislova Street the first important building is the former **Maisel Synagogue [A]**. Constructed in 1590–2 as a triple-naved Renaissance edifice, the synagogue was rebuilt in 1893–1905 in the Neo-Gothic style. On display are metal – especially silver – religious objects from the 17th–19th century, including Torah crowns, shields, mats and indicators (hands), pots, beakers, dishes, candelabras, washing items and tins of spice. By the cashier's desk in the foyer the history of the art of gold and silversmiths is explained.

Silverware in the Maisel Synagogue

On the next corner but one is the **Jewish Town Hall [B]**. Constructed in 1763 and adorned with a wooden tower at about the same time, the synagogue has a Jewish clock; its hands run in the opposite direction. Today the building houses the Senior Rabbinical Council and the administrative offices and assembly chambers of the Jewish community, as well as a kosher restaurant.

The Jewish Town Hall

Beside the Town Hall is the **Town Hall Synagogue [C]**, also known as the High Synagogue, with a rectangular Renaissance Assembly Room. Changing art exhibitions are held here. Opposite stands the most important architectural monument in the former Jewish Quarter: the ★ **Old-New Synagogue** (Staronová synagóga) **[D]**. It was built in 1270 in the Early Gothic style and is thus the oldest remaining synagogue in Europe in which services are still held. A huge banner hangs from the vaulted ceiling; it was presented to the Jews of Prague by Emperor Ferdinand III in recognition of their bravery during the fierce Swedish siege of 1648.

55

The Old-New Synagogue

The synagogue's entrance lobby, a 14th-century addition, had two tills which were used by the tax collectors. From here, women would pass through to the corridors reserved for them, from which they could follow the proceedings in the synagogue through openings in the wall. The synagogue itself was reached through a narrow doorway whose tympanum is decorated with an unusual representation of the Tree of Life.

Inside, the most notable features are the five-section rib vaulting supported by two octagonal pillars; the altar with the Torah shrine on the east wall; the pulpit surrounded by a hand-made, wrought iron balustrade (15th century); and the historic banner of the Prague Jewish community (1357, renewed in 1716).

Outside on the left, at the far end of the U starého hřbitova (the Old Cemetery Alley) stands the **Klausen Synagogue [E]**, a baroque building dating from the end of the 17th century. It was erected on the site of three smaller buildings (a school, a hospital and a prayer hall) and was rebuilt at the end of the 19th century. Today the Klausen Synagogue houses a permanent exhibition of old Hebraic prints and manuscripts.

The Jewish Cemetery

Grave of Rabbi Low

Child's montage, Ceremonial Hall

Near the synagogue is the entrance to the **Old Jewish Cemetery** (Starý židovský hřbitov) **[F]**, established early in the 15th century; the oldest gravestone visible today is dated 1439, the most recent 1787, after which Joseph II forbade burials within densely populated districts of the city. The exact number of gravestones, many of which have disintegrated or sunk into the ground, is unknown, but is estimated to be at least 12,000. Over the centuries, however, it is thought that as many as 200,000 people were buried here.

Most visited is the grave of Rabbi Low (d.1609), which is at the far side of the cemetery, straight ahead from the entrance. The Rabbi is remembered for creating the famous Golem out of clay and bringing it to life. Here, too, is the grave of the Jewish scholar David Oppenheimer (d.1736), an ancestor of Robert Oppenheimer, inventor of the atomic bomb. Near the entrance stands the former **Ceremonial Hall** of the Funeral Brotherhood **[H]**, which contains powerful and moving drawings by children in the Theresienstadt (Terezín) concentration camp.

In the Široka is the **Pinkas Synagogue [G]**, which dates from the 12th century but which was subsequently rebuilt on several occasions. Since 1958 it has served as a poignant memorial to the 77,297 Jews from Bohemia and Moravia who were killed during World War II. Their names are inscribed in alphabetical order around the bare white walls. On the far wall are the names of the notorious death camps.

In order to see the last synagogue, retrace your steps along U starého hřibitova alley, turning right at the end into the Pařížská. The first road on the left (Široká) passes the **Spanish Synagogue [I]**, at present closed for restoration. It was built in 1882–93 in a mock-Moorish style, which accounts for its name.

Route 7

The southwestern section of the Old Town: Small Square – Clam-Gallas Palace – ★ Clementinum – Square of the Crusader Knights – Smetana Museum – Bethlehem Chapel

Depending upon whether you approach this section of the Old Town from the Old Town Square, from Wenceslas Square or from the Charles Bridge, you will come across the sights described below in a different order, and will head for a different orientation point in each case. Those who choose to walk from the Old Town Square to the Charles Bridge (or vice-versa) can take the Karlova and visit the other sights by means of short side-trips or detours. Or the walk could be turned into a round trip.

This route will therefore not describe a fixed itinerary for this section of the city. The individual sights will be listed according to their location, beginning with the Karlova and then describing those which lie to the south, working from west to east. By studying the map on this page, visitors should be able to work out suitable routes, depending on individual taste.

The historic **Small Square** (Malé náměstí) behind the Town Hall, together with the arcades of U radnice (Town Hall Alley) which adjoins it to the north, form one of the most charming sections of the Old Town. The arcades were built during the 14th century; the fountain in the middle,

The Small Square

57

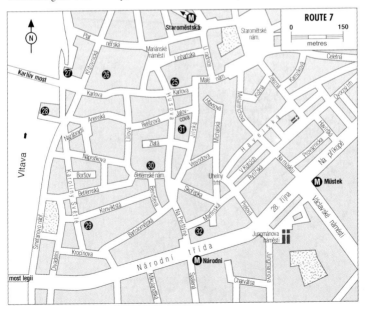

which boasts a fine Renaissance grating, dates from 1550. Many of the houses still bear their old names and signs. Of particular interest is No 12, The Golden Lily, which was built by Christoph Dientzenhofer in 1698, and the house To the Minute, which juts out and forms a link with the Old Town Hall. The latter was built in about 1600 in the Renaissance style and is decorated with attractive *sgraffito* painting.

The Clam-Gallas Palace

The **Clam-Gallas Palace ㉕**, on the corner of Karlova and Husova, is one of the most important baroque buildings in Prague. It was built from 1715 to plans drawn up by Johann Bernhard Fischer von Erlach. The main doorway is supported by the statues of four giants which, together with the additional sculptural decoration, is the work of Matthias Braun. The ceiling fresco inside, which depicts *The Gods on Mount Olympus*, is by Carlo Carlone. Today the building serves as the city archive.

The ★ **Clementinum ㉖**, the famous former Jesuit College, forms the largest complex of buildings in Prague after the castle. The original Dominican monastery on this site was founded during the 13th century but was almost completely destroyed during the Hussite Wars. In 1555, under the direction of the Jesuit Petrus Canisius, work commenced on a complex which was to serve as a Catholic bastion against the Protestant tendencies of the Charles University. The building itself, however, did not really get under way until 1578, when the foundation stone was laid for the Church of the Redeemer (see below), Prague's first Jesuit church. The college building was erected between 1653–1722; it is centred around five courtyards, with study rooms and lecture theatres, libraries, an observatory and

The Clementinum

residential wings. Four libraries are housed on the premises, including the National Library and the University Library.

Four churches are incorporated into the complex. Approached from the Old Town Square along the Karlova, the first one is the Church of St Clement, built in 1711–15, which has a remarkable interior with eight baroque statues by Matthias Bernhard Braun. It is followed by the round Welsh Chapel (1590–1600) and – opposite the Old Town Bridge Tower (*see page 45*) – the **Church of the Redeemer**. This was begun in 1578 and extended in 1643 by a triple-arched porch (with statues by Johann Georg Bendl dating from 1660) and a baroque style interior. In the northeast courtyard stands the Mirror Chapel, dating from 1724, in which exhibitions and concerts are sometimes held.

As a result of its attractive architecture and its magnificent view across the Vltava to Hradčany the charming **Square of the Crusader Knights** (Křižovnické náměstí) has become one of the most popular attractions in the Old Town.

The Church of the Redeemer

Its eastern boundary is formed by the Church of the Redeemer; the northern one by the **Church of the Crusader Knights** , also known as the Church of St Francis, as it is dedicated to St Francis Seraph. The church used to belong to the monastery of the Order of the Knights of the Cross with the Red Star, founded in 1237, whose Grand Masters were the archbishops of Prague between 1561–1694 and were almost permanently at loggerheads with the Jesuits. It was thus intended that the church, built in 1679–89 in accordance with the plans of the French architect Jean-Baptiste Mathey, should be equally as imposing as the Jesuit complex, including the Clementinum and the Church of the Redeemer.

Church of the Crusader Knights

The interior of the church is of interest above all for the vast fresco in the dome; painted by Wenzel Lorenz Reiner in 1722, it portrays *The Last Judgment*. There is also a fine Gloriole (1702) by Matthäus Wenzel Jäckel above the High Altar. Outside, by the right-hand corner of the building, stands the Vintners Column with a statue of St Wenceslas (1676) by Johann Georg Bendel. In front of the church is a neo-Gothic bronze statue of Charles IV (1848) by the Dresden sculptor Ernst Hähnel.

The **Smetana Museum**  (daily except Tuesday 10am–5pm), Novotného lávka 1, is tucked away in a little street jutting out into the Vltava. In this house, decorated with *sgraffito* painting, there is a wealth of exhibits illustrating the life and works of the famous Czech composer Bedřich Smetana (1824–84).

The Smetana Museum

Although not the oldest the **Rotunda of the Holy Cross** (Rotunda sv. Kříže) , Konviktská ulice, erected in about

59

Rotunda of the Holy Cross

Bethlehem Chapel

1100, is undoubtedly the loveliest of the three remaining Romanesque round churches in Prague.

The **Bethlehem Chapel** (Betlémská kaple) **30** is one of the most important sacred monuments in the country. The building dates from 1391; it was here that Jan Hus preached from 1402 until shortly before he moved to Constance (1415). So, too, did Thomas Münzer a few years later, in 1521.

Taken over by the Jesuits in the 17th century, after Protestantism was banned, the chapel was rebuilt, but then demolished in 1786. It was meticulously reconstructed in its original form in 1950–4, partly making use of original building materials. Memorabilia is on display in the adjoining rooms, where Hus actually lived.

The **Church of St Giles** (Kostel sv. Jilji) **31**, also a Hussite place of worship, is a powerful Gothic building, constructed in 1339–71. In 1733 it was rebuilt in the baroque style, probably to plans drawn up by Kilian Ignaz Dientzenhofer. The ceiling frescoes were painted by Wenzel Lorenz Reiner. The interior is dominated by six massive columns dating from the Gothic era; during the 18th century they were clad in reddish-brown marble stucco and adorned with golden capitals.

The **Church of St Martin in the Wall** (Kostel sv. Martina ve zdi) **32**, Martinská ulice, was founded in 1178 and later incorporated into the city wall. The church is important for its historical significance for it was here, in 1414, that Holy Communion 'in both kinds' (bread and wine) was offered for the very first time. Furthermore, various members of the famous family of sculptors, the Brokoffs, are buried here.

Route 8

The New Town to ★★ Vyšehrad: Wenceslas Square – National Museum – Powder Tower – Municipal House – Church of Our Lady of the Snow – ★★ National Theatre – Charles Square – Church of St Carlo Borromeo – Emmaus Monastery – Vyšehrad

Please refer to the maps on pages 12–13 and 65

The focal point of the New Town (Nové Město), and indeed of the entire city, is **Wenceslas Square** (Václavské náměstí). Laid out in 1348 by Charles IV as the Horse Fair in the centre of his New Town, which he himself had established, Wenceslas Square had in those days the same measurements as today: 750m (800yds) long, and only 60m (64yds) wide, which gives it something of the appearance of a street. Closed to motor traffic, Wenceslas Square is the city's favourite place for a stroll. Nowhere else will you find so many hotels, restaurants, shops, cinemas, cafés, bars and nightclubs as here. Many are hidden away in passageways or houses with public thoroughfares.

Lining both sides of the square are a number of magnificent art nouveau buildings (*see also page 77*), including the venerable Grand Hotel Evropa, the Palais Alfa, Peterka House and the Palais Koruna.

At the top end of the square, forming a monumental boundary, is the **National Museum** (Národní muzeum) ❸, built in 1885–90 in neo-Renaissance style (daily except Tuesday from 9am, Monday and Friday until 4pm, Wednesday, Thursday, Saturday and Sunday until 5pm). The entire external and internal design was planned with the intention of creating here the intellectual centre of the nation, and thus includes vast sculptures and paintings portraying the most important events in the country's history. The museum possesses a valuable library with some 1,000,000 volumes and 8,000 manuscripts.

The exhibition galleries are grouped around a Hall of Fame surmounted by a vast dome. The museum, which is well worth visiting, includes the following sections: natural sciences, early history, coins, archaeology, mineralogy, geology and palaeontology as well as drama.

In 1912, following 30 years of preparatory work, the **Monument to St Wenceslas** by the sculptor Josef Myslbek was erected in front of the museum. It is considered to be a supreme example of the artistic style of the time. To the left of the museum stands the steel-and-glass Czech National Assembly Building.

In the middle of Wenceslas Square is a memorial to the student Jan Palach, who committed suicide by setting fire to himself as a protest in 1969. At the lower end of the square, turn right into the main street **Na Příkopě**,

Wenceslas Square

The National Museum

Wenceslas Monument

whose name recalls the fact that it was laid out along the former moat between the Old and the New Town, which was filled in in 1781. On the right is the Sylvia-Tarouca Palace (No 12), built in 1670 and reconstructed in 1748, then, on the corner of the Panská ulice, the Church of the Holy Cross dating from 1816. Finally, No 22 is the Příchovský Palace, built in the 18th century and from 1875 known as the German House. It has now been rechristened the Slovanský dům, the Slavic House.

A little further on the left is the **Powder Tower 34** (Prašná brána), built in 1475 by Mattias Rejsek as the East Gate of the Old Town. Here, near the royal town palace (see below), began the Royal Way, along which the coronation procession of the kings of Bohemia passed on their way to Hradčany. The route led along the Celetná, across the Old Town Square, the Charles Bridge and the Lesser Quarter Square up to St Vitus' Cathedral. In 1757, during the Seven Years' War, the tower was attacked by the Prussians and badly damaged: in 1875–86 it was rebuilt in neo-Gothic style. Inside can be seen parts of the original form. The tower, which affords a fine view of the city, received its present name during the 18th century, when gunpowder was stored here.

The Municipal House

The tower is directly linked to the **Municipal House** (Obecni dům), also known as the House of Representation **35**, built in 1906–11 in art nouveau style on the site occupied between 1380–1547 by the Royal Court, the king's city residence which at that time was more important than Hradčany. It was here that the Czechoslovak Republic was proclaimed on 28 October 1918. The Municipal House has splendid interior decorations, but is closed for renovation at present.

Returning along Na příkopě to Wenceslas Square, the route continues along 28 October Street (Ulice 28. října) (*see Maps pages 12–13*). A short distance on the left is Jungmann Square (Jungmannovo náměstí), named after the Czech linguist and Enlightenment scholar Josef Jungmann (1773–1847). Here you should pass directly through the gateway to the Franciscan Presbytery to the **Church of Our Lady of the Snows** (Kostel Panny Marie Sněžné) **36**, one of the most interesting Gothic churches in Prague. Founded in 1347 by Charles IV, it was originally planned to be even larger than St Vitus' Cathedral. During the Hussite Wars, however, building came to a standstill. The choir, the only part of the building to have been completed by that time, collapsed during the 16th century; in 1601 it was rebuilt to its original height of 35m (112ft). No one can fail to be impressed by the sheer height of the single-nave, pillarless interior. The most important feature is the High Altar: created from 1625 onwards by several artists it is the largest altar in the city.

Our Lady of the Snows

The National Theatre

This church played a significant role in Czech history: from here, the Hussite preacher Jan Zelivsky and his followers set off to march to the New Town Hall (*see page 64*), an act which led to the First Defenestration of Prague and the start of the Hussite Wars.

If you continue from Jungmann Square along the same street, which is now known as Národni třída (National Street), you will arrive in front of the ★★ **National Theatre** (Národni divadlo) ⓷ on the banks of the Vltava. The building represents the supreme achievement of 19th-century Bohemian architecture. Building commenced in 1868, and was financed entirely by private donations from the Czech people. Designed by Josef Zítek, the theatre was inaugurated on 15 June 1881 with a performance of Smetana's *Libuše*. Two months later the building was burned to the ground, but was restored with the aid of endowments and donations and re-opened in 1883.

Sculptures on the theatre

Like the National Museum, which was built somewhat later, the National Theatre was planned from the start as a symbol of the revived Czech national awareness, and as a counterbalance to the city's numerous German-speaking theatres. The sculptures and paintings were planned with this aim in mind.

From this point, the most Legií bridge (Bridge of Legions) leads across the Vltava to join Vitězná Street. Turning south along the esplanade, however, leads to the setting of the Slavic Congress in 1848: the Slavic Island (Slovanský ostrov). The island, where there are boats for hire, is also known as Sophie Island because it is the setting for the Sophie Concert Hall, where, among others, Berlioz, Liszt and Wagner performed.

Boating on the Vltava

Shortly before reaching the end of the island, turn left into the Myslíkova ulice, following the direction of the tram lines, before forking diagonally right into Odborů and continuing to **Charles Square** (Karlovo náměstí), which – like Wenceslas Square – was laid out by Charles IV in 1348, but this one was to be city's cattle market. It has retained its original proportions: 530m (565yds) by 150m (160yds).

The New Town Hall

On the north side stands the **New Town Hall** (Novoměstská radnice) **❸❺**, also of historic interest. Built in 1374–1498 in Gothic style, the Town Hall was rebuilt in Renaissance style in 1526 and then reconstructed in 1900. This was the arena for the First Defenestration of Prague on 30 July 1419. Led by the Premonstratensian priest Jan Zelivský, a procession of Hussite supporters gathered at the Church of Our Lady of the Snows with the intention of demanding the release from prison of their fellow-Hussites. When their request was greeted with scorn (some say also with stones), the enraged crowd threw the town councillors from the window and lynched them. This incident provoked the outbreak of the Hussite Wars, which were to continue for 15 years.

64

In the southern section of the square, the east side is occupied by the former Jesuit College and the **Church of St Ignatius ❸❾**. The collegiate building was constructed over a period of many years beginning in 1659 to complement the Clementinum in the Old Town (*see page 58*). The church itself was built between 1665–99.

From the middle of Charles Square, take Resslova Street towards the Vltava; on the right, at the junction with Na Zderaze, is the former **Church of St Carlo Borromeo ❹❶**, built in the 1730s. Now known as the Church of St Cyril and St Methodius (Kostel sv. Cyrila a Metoděje), it serves as the cathedral of the Czech Orthodox Church.

On 18 June 1942, the church was the scene of an unequal struggle between the assassins of Reichsprotector Heydrich and the SS. The assassins, who had hidden in the crypt, were betrayed, and the SS surrounded the church with 350 men. Despite their efforts, it took them six hours to force their way in, at the cost of 14 lives and dozens of injuries. But they failed to take a single captive because everyone had either been killed or committed suicide. Today the crypt has been converted into a memorial museum, decorated with photos, documents and memorabilia (Monday to Friday 9–11am).

In the crypt of St Carlo Borromeo

For the rest of the route it is recommended that you study the map opposite. Leaving the church, head for the southern end of Charles Square, where, at No 40, stands the so-called **Faust House** (Faustův dům) **❹❶**, whose history stretches back into the 14th century. The building acquired its baroque appearance during the 18th century, when it belonged to alchemist Count Ferdinand Mladota, but 200 years earlier it was the home of Edward Kelly, the Englishman employed by Rudolf II to search for the Philosopher's Stone. Today it is a chemist's shop.

Following the tram lines in a southerly direction along Vyšehradska, you will come to the **Church of St John of Nepomuk on the Rock** (Kostel sv. Jana na skalce) **42**, built in 1730 by Kilian Ignaz Dientzenhofer. The dome fresco (1748) by Karel Kovár depicts the church's patron being accepted into the congregation of saints.

Opposite stands the **Emmaus Monastery** (Klášter na Slovanech) **43**, founded in 1347 for Benedictine monks of the Slavic Ritual. The complex was badly damaged during an air raid on 14 February 1945. Of great artistic merit are the Gothic frescoes, dating from about 1360, in the cloister, some of which were destroyed. Some 80 paintings spread across the 26 wall sections portray the Life and Passion of Christ together with introductory scenes from the Old Testament. The reconstruction of the former monastery church was completed in 1968 with the addition of two modern towers.

Following the tram route southwards, the Botanical Gardens of Prague will be seen on the left. Turning into Na slupi and bearing right through the tram crossing and then left uphill via Lumirova or Přemyslova you will eventually reach the ★★ **Vyšehrad**, the rock jutting out high above the Vltava which is regarded as the place where the city of Prague really began. It is believed that the leg-

Views of Church of St John of Nepomuk on the Rock

65

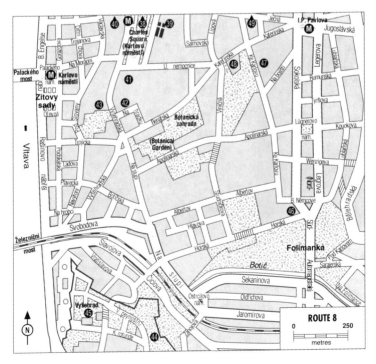

Rotunda of St Martin

Bust of Dvořák

Interior of Charles Palace

endary Princess Libuše, at the beginning of the 9th century, prophesied that a great city would be founded here. Between the 10th and 12th centuries, Vyšehrad was the political and religious centre of the country, then it was replaced by Hradčany, and most of its old glory paled.

Passing through the Tabor Gate (1655) and the Leopold Gate (1670), the visitor enters the former castle compound. On the right stands the **Rotunda of St Martin** (Rotunda sv. Martina) **44**, dating from the end of the 11th century and one of the three remaining Romanesque round churches in Prague.

After passing the rotunda, turn left off the main road to reach the southern part of the former fortifications, with a particularly fine view of the Vltava and the pleasure marina. Nearby is the neo-Gothic Church of St Peter and St Paul **45**, built in 1885–1903. Adjoining the church is the Memorial Cemetery and the celebrated Slavín Mausoleum; many famous Czechs are buried here, including the composers Smetana (whose tombstone is in the form of an obelisk) and Dvořák (bust), as well as the writers Čapek and Neruda.

Vyšehrad can also be reached by underground; it is ten minutes' walk from the station of the same name.

Leave the Vyšehrad by means of Pevnostni Street, which leads through a monumental gateway, crossing back above the railway and then along Horská Street up to **Charles Palace** (Karlov) **46**. The eccentric central building, in the middle of a large courtyard, was founded in 1350 by Charles IV and dedicated by him to his personal patron and namesake, Charlemagne. The Palatinate Chapel in Aachen served as model for the octagonal ground plan. The present vaulting was added in 1575, and during the 18th century the interior was remodelled in baroque style. The replica of the Santa Scala in Rome was also added at that time.

Leaving the church, continue along Ke Karlovu in a northerly direction. At No 20 is the **Villa Amerika 47**, a delightful summer palace built by Kilian Ignaz Dientzenhofer in 1717–20 for Count Michna. It acquired its present name during the 19th century in honour of an inn of that name which stood here. Today the Villa Amerika houses the interesting **Dvořák Museum** (daily except Monday 10am–5pm).

To the west, in Kateřinská Street, is the **Church of St Catherine 48**, founded by Charles IV in 1354 and rebuilt in 1737–41. The church has an elegant, octagonal steeple, but is not open to the public. From here, follow Lipová and Stepánská back to Wenceslas Square, noticing on the right the **Church of St Stephen 49** (1351). Opposite, in the courtyard, is the Rotunda of St Longinus, one of the city's three Romanesque round churches.

Additional Sights

Listed below are some of the city's additional sights which lie off the routes described so far (*see Map, pages 12–13*).

The **Petřín Hill** lies above the Lesser Quarter. It makes a pleasant excursion and can be reached on foot from Strahov Monastery (*see page 38*), from the Lesser Quarter Square or from Karmelitská and Újezd streets. From the latter you can also take the funicular railway. In the southwest, Petřín Hill is bordered by the Hunger Wall, erected by Charles IV in 1360–2 during a famine, when the labourers were paid in food.

On the summit of Petřín Hill stands the charming twin-towered Church of St Lawrence (Kostel sv Vavřince) **50**, built between 1735–70. Somewhat further away stands the **Observation Tower 51** (daily except Monday 9.30am–5pm), built in 1891 in imitation of the Eiffel Tower in Paris. It is 60m (192ft) high and affords a breathtaking panorama of the city for those who are prepared to negotiate the 299 steps.

Observation Tower

On the slopes are pretty gardens leading down towards the Lesser Quarter: the Seminar Garden **52**, the Schönborn Garden **53** and the Lobkowitz Garden **54**. (The latter two are not open to the public as they form part of the embassies of the USA and Germany). To the south lies the **Kinsky Garden 55** and the Kinsky Summer Palace, which contains the Ethnographic Museum (Národopisné muzeum), closed at present for renovation.

Gardens on Petřín Hill

67

It is worth descending from Petřín Hill northwards via Vlašská Street, passing the Welsh Hospital **56**, erected in 1602, and (at No 19) the Lobkowitz Palace **57**, built in 1703–7 and extended by the addition of another storey in 1769. Today this splendid baroque palace houses the German Embassy.

On the way down from Petřín Hill

The **Villa Bertramka** ❸, Smíchov, Mozartova 2 (tram 4, 7, 9; underground station Anděl) will forever be linked with the name of Wolfgang Amadeus Mozart. In 1787 Mozart lived in this summer villa, the property of the Dušeks, who were both musicians. At the time the villa lay well outside the city limits. During this period, the composer completed his opera *Don Giovanni*. He was to stay here again in 1789, and in 1791, when he composed his opera *La Clemenzia di Tito*. In 1929 the house was transformed into a memorial museum (daily 9.30am–6pm). Concerts are also held here on a regular basis, and during the Mozart Festival (*see page 82*).

Bronze doors

Lying in the east of the city, **Vitkov Hill** ❺ can be reached from the Powder Tower via Hybernská and Husitská streets (near the main railway station). Immediately after the railway bridge, by the Museum of Military History, turn left uphill into U památníku.

On the hill stands the National Memorial (Národní památník), a massive cube covered with granite slabs, built in 1928–38 to symbolise the struggle for independence and containing the Tomb of the Unknown Soldier. The bronze doors depict the struggles of May 1945.

Statue of Jan Žižka

In front of the monument stands a bronze equestrian statue 9m (29ft) high, 10m (32ft) long and 5m (16ft) wide of the Hussite leader Jan Žižka, who repulsed the attacking forces of Emperor Sigismund from this spot on 14 July 1420. Created by Bohumil Kafka in 1950, it weighs 16.5 tonnes and is claimed to be the largest equestrian statue in the world.

To gain further insight into the history of the city, a visit to the **Museum of the City of Prague** (Muzeum hlavního města Prahy) ❻ (daily except Monday 10am–12.30pm and 1.30–6pm) is highly recommended. It is located in Svermovy Sady, at the end of Na pofíčí (nearest underground station: Florenc). The museum's rich collections provide a survey of the development of Prague from the earliest times until the present day. Valuable works of art and a detailed model of the city by A Langweil (1830) are among the exhibits.

The impressive neo-Renaissance building of the ★ **State Opera** (Státní Opera) ❻ stands on Wilsonova Street between the National Museum and the main railway station. Dating from 1886–8, it has one of the loveliest auditoriums in Europe. Designed in rococo style in white and gold, the hall is also renowned for its excellent acoustics. Some ballets are performed here, as well as opera. (Advance ticket sales: Monday to Friday 10am–6pm, Saturday and Sunday 10am–5pm; tel: 26 53 53.)

★ **St Agnes' Convent** (Klášter sv. Anežky) ❻ (daily except Monday, 10am–6pm), Anežská Street, is situated on the northern outskirts of the Old Town near the Vltava.

The convent was founded in 1234 by Agnes, the sister of Wenceslas I; it was later extended to include a Franciscan monastery and seven churches.

Closed in 1797, the convent represents the most important Early Gothic building in Prague. It rapidly fell to ruin, however, and large sections were totally destroyed. For decades restoration work has been proceeding to protect the remaining three churches and the principal convent buildings. Particular value is being attached to the restoration of the sections dating from the 13th and 14th century. Within the sections of the convent complex where restoration work is complete there are two collections belonging to the National Gallery: Czech painting of the 19th and 20th century and 19th-century handicrafts.

In the north of the city, near the zoo, is the ★ **Troja Palace** (Trojsky Zámek: April to December Tuesday to Sunday 10am–5pm; otherwise Saturday only 10am–4pm). It was built in baroque style by Jean-Baptiste Mathey for Count Sternberg in 1679–85, and is famous for the staircase on the garden side, with statues representing the Titans' struggle against the gods on Mount Olympus. The palace also includes the Imperial Hall, with a large ceiling fresco (1691–7) by Abraham Godyn representing homage to the House of Habsburg, and a gallery of 19th-century Bohemian painting.

The **Star Summer Palace** (Letohrádek Hvězda: daily except Monday, 10am–5pm), set in a landscaped garden in the west of the city (tram no 1, 2, 18), was built in 1555–8 for Archduke Ferdinand of Tyrol, who occasionally visited Prague. The ground plan is in the shape of a six-pointed star. The interior has fine stucco ceilings and houses a museum dedicated to the writer Alois Jirásek (1851–1930) and the artist Mikolás Aleš (1852–1913).

The **Pilgrimage Church on the White Mountain** is situated in the west of Prague, at the terminus Bílá hora of tram no 22 from the National Theatre. The site of the decisive victory of the Catholic army over the Protestant forces in 1620 is marked by a little pilgrimage church surrounded by an ambulatory with four corner chapels, dating from the first quarter of the 18th century. The dome frescoes are the work of Cosmas Damian Asam, Johann Adam Schöpf and Wenzel Lorenz Reiner.

Břevnov Monastery, in the Prague suburb of the same name, can be reached by tram no 8 or 22. It was founded in 993 by St Adalbert of Prague as the first monastery in Bohemia, and was run by the Benedictine order. Remains of a Romanesque basilica have been discovered. The present buildings (1708–40), of which only the church is open to the public (daily 10am–5pm), were largely the work of Christoph Dientzenhofer; his son Kilian Ignaz was responsible for the interior.

Helpful hints

Karlstein Castle and battlements

Excursions from Prague

With the aid of the following descriptions of sights near Prague and the map on page 11 you should be able to draw up routes to match your own particular interests.

It is also possible to join one of the day trips organised by ČEDOK or one of the other travel agents (*see pages 98–9 for more details*).

★★ Karlstejn (Karlstein)

Karlštejn/Karlstein, 28km/ 17 miles from Prague, is the most attractive castle in Bohemia and as such the most rewarding destination for a day trip.

If travelling by car, leave Prague on the E12 in the direction of Pilsen, and take the Loděnice exit.

Karlštejn can also be reached by train, from Smichovské (Metro Smíchovské nádrazi). Trains depart more or less every hour and the journey takes about 25 minutes. It will take approximately 30 minutes to reach the castle from the station or slightly less from the car park.

The castle is open daily except Monday and on the day after a public holiday as follows: March, November and December 9am–3pm; April, May, September, October 9am–4pm; June, July, August 8am–5pm. It is closed at lunchtime each day from 12 noon–12.30pm. Conducted tours are compulsory and last approximately one hour. The last tour begins one hour before the castle closes. Tickets are available in the Outer Courtyard [B].

Charles IV had the castle built in 1348–65 by two of the most important architects of the Gothic Age, Matthew of Arras and Peter Parler, who were also responsible for St Vitus' Cathedral in

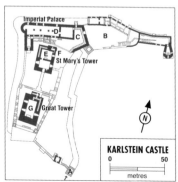

Imperial Palace

D
C
B
E F
St Mary's Tower

G
Great Tower

N

KARLSTEIN CASTLE
0   50
metres

A

Prague. Here – far from the capital and impregnable against outside attack – the emperor planned to keep the Imperial Jewels, the Coronation Insignia of the Bohemian Kings and the relics he had gathered together from all over Europe. The pious ruler, who was also a noted theological scholar, planned to meditate in peace surrounded by his religious treasures.

From the Entrance [A], the tour proceeds underneath the castle to the Outer Courtyard [B], which also serves as an open-air theatre. Crossing the Inner Courtyard [C] it then ascends to the ★ Imperial Palace [D].

There are five rooms on two floors which house a large number of exhibits, the positioning of which is not yet final. At present, the first floor contains a number of architectural models, remains of the stained glass windows of the Chapel of the Cross [G] and two wooden statues (Ss Catherine and Nicholas) dating from the beginning of the 15th century. On the second floor are the remains of a glass painting from the Chapel of St Catherine [F], a lovely diptych dating from the second half of the 14th century, casts of the busts in the triforium of St Vitus' Cathedral, plans and photocopies. Of the private quarters of Charles IV on the second floor, only the Audience Room has survived.

Statue of St Catherine

The tour continues through St Mary's Tower, where there is a **Chapel of the Virgin Mary** divided into two sections [E], in which remains of the original frescoes (including the Horseman of the Apocalypse and a number of likenesses of Charles IV) can still be seen. Of particular interest is the room next door, the little Chapel of St Catherine [F]. This was the emperor's private chapel, which no one but he was allowed to enter. He often shut himself in here for days at a time; food and important documents were passed to him through a narrow opening at floor level.

Chapel of the Virgin Mary: details

The walls are decorated with approximately 1,000 semi-precious stones set in gold. On the altar, at eye level for the kneeling emperor, are portrayed Christ, the Virgin Mary and St John with companions. Above, in the altar niche, is the Virgin Mary with the Infant Jesus, to whom Charles IV and his third wife, Anna von Schweidnitz, are paying homage.

A drawbridge used to lead from St Mary's Tower to the Great Tower, which contained the holy of holies, the ★ **Chapel of the Cross** [G]. This chapel is not open to the public; visitors must be content with video pictures of the interior.

The chapel, completed in 1365, was planned as a single vast treasure chamber, with decorations of artistic and material value corresponding to its precious contents. The twin-trussed chapel is divided by a gilt screen. The

The Chapel of St Catherine

ribbed vaulting is also covered in gold set with stars of molten glass. The walls are set with 2,451 precious and semi-precious stones, including topazes, amethysts, jasper, onyx and chrysolite. No fewer than 1,300 golden thorns encircle the room like a ribbon, on which the candles shine. Through the quartz window, only subdued light from outside was able to penetrate. Master Theodorich, the most important Bohemian artist of the time, painted 127 exquisite portraits of saints, behind which the relics collected by the emperor were kept. He also painted the Crucifixion scene on the High Altar. Behind the golden screen beneath were the coronation insignia and the most important relics. During the Middle Ages only the emperor, the archbishop and a few privileged people were permitted to enter the room. Even today, the chapel is only open to the public to a very restricted extent.

Zbraslav

Zbraslav lies 10km (6 miles) south of Prague. The present buildings of the Cistercian abbey, founded in 1291 and destroyed in 1420 by the Hussites, date from 1716. Today they house the National Gallery collection of Czech sculptures from the 18th–20th centuries (daily except Monday 10am–6pm). Also worth visiting is the 17th-century baroque church.

Transport alternatives

★ Konopišté

Konopišté is 42km (26 miles) southeast of Prague, near Benešov. It can be reached by train from the Wilsonova station to Benešov, then a short bus ride. This magnificent castle, dating from the 14th century, belonged to a number of aristocratic families before it was purchased in 1894 by the heir to the throne of Austria-Hungary, Archduke Francis Ferdinand, whose assassination on 28 June 1914 was the direct cause of World War I. He had it rebuilt and fitted out at enormous cost. In 82 rooms there are collections of weapons, paintings and sculptures, including a many of portraits of St George, in whom the Archduke was particularly interested. There are also a large number of valuable furnishings, dating especially from the 17th and 18th century and some 300,000 hunting trophies – of which, however, only 3,000 are on display.

In the bedroom of Admiral Tirpitz is a Late Gothic lindenwood sculpture, The Burial of Christ, and in the bedroom of William II there is a Florentine portrait of the Madonna, both dating from the 15th century. In the Castle Chapel, which Francis Ferdinand had restored in neo-Gothic style for the sum of 300,000 Austrian guilders, hang a number of valuable German and Italian panel paintings, wooden reliefs and winged altars. The castle park is also very attractive.

Orlík

The history of the castle at Orlík, 80km (50 miles) south of Prague on the Vltava, reaches back into the 13th century. It was subsequently rebuilt and extended on a number of occasions. Since 1717 the castle has been in the possession of the princes of Schwarzenberg, who have embellished it with precious works of art. The castle was almost completely destroyed by fire in 1802, but it was quickly repaired and rebuilt. It has been administered by the state since 1948. Of particular interest are the Blue Drawing Room on the first floor and the Empire-style salons on the second floor.

North of Orlík, the Vltava is dammed by a barrage. This means that the castle no longer lies as far above the water table as it once did. You can take a motor boat across the reservoir to Zvíkov (12km/ 7 miles). There are also facilities for bathing and water sports.

Boating on the reservoir

Zvíkov

Zvíkov/Klingenberg, 92km (58 miles) from Prague, stands at the confluence of the Otava and the Vltava. The castle, erected during the 13th century by Přemysl Otakar I and King Wenceslas I, stands on a high cliff. The oldest section is the Markoman Tower, which owes its name to the fact that the Markomans originally resided here. Of particular note are the Early Gothic arcaded courtyard and the lovely frescoes.

From Zvíkov it's only 30km (19 miles) to Tabor, which has a Late Gothic Town Hall and attractive old streets.

Lidice

Lidice, 25km (15 miles) west of Prague, lies south of the road to Slaný. This village is where the Nazis wreaked revenge for the assassination of Deputy Reichsprotektor Reinhard Heydrich. During the night of 10 June 1942, the 192 male inhabitants were shot; the women were taken to the concentration camp at Ravensbrück, where 60 of them were tortured to death. The 105 children from Lidice were taken to Lodz, from where the majority were sent to an extermination camp. The site of the former village has been turned into a poignant memorial to the victims of the massacre.

Countryside near Lidice

Finally, a few other potential excursion destinations: the 13th-century royal castle of Křivoklát 50km (31 miles) west of Prague; the stalactite caves near Koněprusy 40km (25 miles) from Prague; the beautiful, medieval mountain town ★ Kutná Hora/ Kuttenberg 64km (40 miles) east of Prague; and the wine-growing area and castle of ★ Mělník 30km (19 miles) north of Prague, at the confluence of the Vltava and the Elbe.

73

Art History

Architecture

After years of painstaking restoration, important architectural sites such as the Old Town Square have now been returned to their former glory. Today, Prague is a living architectural museum, where all phases of development are vividly documented, from early, Romanesque origins, to mighty Gothic churches and monasteries, splendid baroque palaces and magnificent art nouveau boulevards and buildings created at the end of the last century and the early years of the present one.

The dates quoted in brackets after the buildings listed below refer to the year of commencement.

The Romanesque era
On Hradčany will be found the remains of St Mary's Church (c 875), the old Church of St George (915–20), St Vitus' Rotunda (926), St Vitus' Basilica (1061) and the Romanesque Royal Palace (11–12th century). The rotundas of St Martin, St Longinus and the Holy Cross all date from about 1100. Prague's most important Romanesque building is St George's Basilica, which was rebuilt in 1142.

The Gothic era
The Convent of St Agnes (c 1234), the Old New Synagogue (c 1270), what constitutes today the middle storey of the Royal Palace (c 1270), the Old Town Hall (1338) and the Church of St Giles (1339) all date from the early Gothic era.

Matthew of Arras began the construction of St Vitus' Cathedral (1344) and Karlstein Castle (1348); after his death, the work was continued by Peter Parler (1330–99). He and his pupils were responsible for, among other things, the Wenceslas Chapel (1362), the busts on the triforium (1374) and the tombs of the Přemyslids (1376) in St Vitus' Cathedral, as well as the Charles Bridge (1357) and the Old Town Bridge Tower (c 1375).

Also dating from the 14th century are the Church of Our Lady of the Snows (1347), the Emmaus Monastery (1347), the Karlshof (1350), the Týn Church (1365), the oriel chapel of the Carolinum (c 1370), the New Town Hall (1374), the oriel chapel of the Old Town Hall (1381), and the Hall of Pillars of Wenceslas IV (c 1400).

Later works include the Lesser Quarter Bridge Tower (1464) and the Powder Tower (1475). In about 1500, Late Gothic art in Prague reached its zenith under Benedikt Ried, who created the upper storey of the Royal Palace (including the Vladislav Hall, the Knights' Staircase and the Louis Wing) as well as the Vladislav Oratorium (1493) in St Vitus' Cathedral.

The Old Town Square

75

Our Lady of the Snows

Deserving of mention in the realm of painting are the Hohenfurth Altar (c 1350), the Altar of the Master of Wittingau (c 1380) (both on display in St George's Monastery on Hradčany, which forms part of the National Gallery, *see page 30*), the panel pictures (c 1360) of Master Theodorich in Karlstejn Castle and the frescoes (c 1360) in the Emmaus Monastery.

The Renaissance

Representative of this era are the Belvedere summer palace (1534), the Schwarzenberg Palace (1543), the Star Castle (or Hunting Lodge) (1555), the Church of the Redeemer (1578), the Spanish Room and the Rudolf Gallery (1589) in Hradčany Castle, as well as the windows (1493) of the Vladislav Hall, the south portal (1510–20) of St George's Church and, in St Vitus' Cathedral, the organ loft (1559–61) and the Royal Crypt (1564–89).

Cathedral organ loft

The baroque era

The era of baroque architecture begins in Prague with the Church of Our Lady of Victory (1611) and the Matthias Gate (1614), followed by – to name but a few examples – the Waldstein Palace (1623), the Church of St Ignatius (1665) and the Czernín Palace (1669). The French architect Jean-Baptiste Mathey (1630–95) was responsible for designing the Church of the Crusader Knights (1679), the Troja Palace (1679), the Riding School (1679) and the Tuscan Palace (1695).

During the first half of the 18th century, Christoph Dientzenhofer (1655–1722) and his son Kilian Ignaz (1689–1751) had a profound effect on the city's architecture, both designing new buildings and converting existing ones. Dientzenhofer the Elder began the construction of the Church of St Nicholas in the Lesser Quarter (1703), the Břevnov Monastery (1708) and the Loreto Shrine (1717); his son continued the work. The latter was also responsible for the Villa Amerika (1717), the Church of St John of Nepomuk on the Rock (1730) and the Church of St Nicholas in the Old Town (1732). Anselmo Lurago was the architect of the Church of the Holy Cross (1763); Johann Bernhard Fischer von Erlach (1656–1723) produced the sketches for the Clam-Gallas Palace and the tombs of St John of Nepomuk (St Vitus' Cathedral) and Count Mitrowitz (St James's).

Ceiling frescoes, St Nicholas

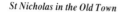

St Nicholas in the Old Town

Important baroque painters were Karel Škréta (1610–74), Johann Peter Brandl (1668–1735), Wenzel Lorenz Reiner (1689–1743) and Johann Lukas Kracker (1717–79); the most famous baroque sculptors were Johann Georg Bendl (1630–80), Matthäus Wenzel Jäckel (1655–1738), Ferdinand Maximilian Brokoff (1688–1731) and Matthias Bernhard Braun (1684–1738).

Art nouveau in Prague

A Prague institution

At the beginning of the 20th century, art nouveau architecture blosssomed in Prague. Alphons Mucha (1860–1939), who achieved international recognition for the posters he designed for the actress Sarah Bernhardt, lived and worked in the city. Czech art nouveau drew its greatest inspiration from Paris, and most Prague artists visited the French capital, in addition to the other great artistic centres of the time, notably Vienna and Berlin. Nonetheless, art nouveau in Prague developed into an independent form of artistic expression, as witnessed by numerous architectural elements that can still be seen today. A splendid example of the genre is the Municipal House by Osvald Polívka and Antonín Balšánek near the Powder Tower. The Grand Hotel Evropa and the Peterka House, both on Wenceslas Square, were designed by Jan Kotěra, a pupil of the Viennese architect Otto Wagner. The Svatopluk Čech Bridge by Koula and the magnificent facades of Pařížka street form a remarkable urban ensemble of art nouveau architecture.

Art nouveau detail

Literature

Franz Kafka (1883–1924) spent most of his life in Prague. He was born in the house called The Tower (commemorative plaque *see page 53*) by the Church of St Nicholas in the Old Town. From 1889–93 he attended the primary school on the Meat Market, in 1893–1901 the Old Town German State Grammar School in the Kinsky Palace and in 1901–6 the Charles University, where he gained a doctorate in law. From 1907–8 he worked for the Assicurazioni Generali on Wenceslas Square, and from 1908 until he retired in 1922 in the Establishment for Workers' Accident Insurance at Na poříčí 7.

Kafka lived with his parents for most of his life, at several different addresses in the city. During the winter of 1916–17 he worked during the evenings and at night in the cottage of his favourite sister Ottla in the Golden Lane in Hradčany (*see page 30*). During the spring of 1917 he also rented for a while a two-room flat in the Schönborn Palace, which today is the US Embassy.

After his death in a sanatorium in Kierling near Klosterneuburg, Kafka was buried in the New Jewish Cemetery (Nový židovský hřbitov), in the east of the city, where his parents were later also buried.

Kafka is best known for his novels *The Trial* and *The Castle*, both published after his death, and both of which depict confused, alienated individuals when faced with bureaucratic authority.

Egon Erwin Kisch

Egon Erwin Kisch (1885–1948), the 'roving reporter', was born and lived for many years in the house called 'The Two Bears' (*see page 49*), now a museum; his father had a draper's shop on the ground floor.

Rainer Maria Rilke (1875–1926) was born at Jindřišská ulice 19, opposite the main post office. At the age of 11 he was sent to the military secondary school at St Pölten. Between 1892–6 he attended grammar school in Prague once more. In 1896 his first works were published there: the *Larenopfer*, an anthology of poems about Prague and other Bohemian subjects. After 1896 he returned to Prague only for brief visits.

The House of the Two Bears

Franz Werfel (1890–1945) was born at what is now known as Opletalova ulice 41. He also lived there for most

of the time until he was called up for military service in the Austrian army in 1915.

Of the many other German-speaking writers whose names are closely linked with the city, it will suffice to mention Gustav Meyrink (1868–1932), the editor of the book *The Golem*, and Max Brod (1884–1968), Kafka's friend and literary executor.

Virtually all important Czech writers of the late 19th and early 20th centuries lived in Prague for a considerable part of their lives. They include the Romantic lyric poet Karel Hynek Mácha (1810–36), whose epic poem *May* (1836) is regarded as one of the milestones in modern Czech poetry; the collector of Czech folk songs and fairy tales, Karel Jaromir Erben (1811–70); and Božena Němková (1820–62), the author of the novel *Grandmother*. There are three others who have achieved greater fame beyond the boundaries of their native country.

Jan Neruda's grave

Jan Neruda (1834–91) compiled the *Tales of the Lesser Quarter*, a collection of novellas and partly humourous, partly reflective sketches from the Malá Strana. He lived for many years in the house called The Two Suns (*see page 42*) in the street now named Nerudova in his honour. He was a disciple of Romanticism but developed into the foremost classical poet in modern Czech literature.

The Two Suns

Jaroslav Hašek (1882–1923), a compulsive and accomplished hoaxer and practical joker, achieved world fame as the author of *The Good Soldier Schweik*, a brilliantly incisive satire on military life, and still the best-known book in the Czech language. Schweik, an irresponsible and undisciplined drunkard, liar and scrounger, is widely thought to be at least partly autobiographical in inspiration. Having deserted the Austrian army in 1915, he crossed over to the Russian side, but managed to make satirical attacks on both régimes. His favourite pub, U kalicha (The Chalice), is a great tourist attraction today (*see page 88*). Hašek, almost an exact contemporary of Franz Kafka, was born at Školská ulice 16, where there is a commemorative plaque.

Karel Čapek (1890–1938), the novelist and playwright, lived and died at Ulice Bratří Čapků in the Vinohrady district. He was the son of a country doctor, who was a friend of the president, TG Masaryk. His best plays describe the problems of a centrally organised machine age. His play *RUR*, first performed in 1921, invented the word 'robot'. The plot deals with the construction of a man-like machine which functioned more reliably than a man.

More recent Czech-born writers include Jaroslav Seifert, who was awarded the Nobel prize for literature in 1984; Milan Kundera, famous for *The Unbearable Lightness of Being* (1984); Ivan Klima, born in 1931; and, of course, the president, Václav Havel.

The Estates Theatre

Music and Theatre

Music

Musical tradition in Bohemia stretches right back to the Early Middle Ages, but it wasn't until the 19th century, after the reawakening of the Czech national consciousness, that Czech composers and their music were able to assert themselves in their home country. Until then, many musicians had little alternative but to emigrate, to cities like Vienna, Paris and Rome, and their place was taken in Prague by a long line of illustrious visitors.

Wolfgang Amadeus Mozart (1756–91) came to Prague for the first time on 11 January 1787, and was greeted with rapturous applause at a performance of the *Marriage of Figaro* in the Nostiz Theatre, today the Estates Theatre (*see page 48*). He lived in an inn, The Golden Angel at Celetná ulice 588, which no longer exists, and in the palace of Count Thun, today the British Embassy. On 14 January he wrote in a letter: 'Here, people talk about nothing except *Figaro*, which is certainly a great honour for me.' The director of the theatre, Bondini, commissioned him to write an opera for a fee of 100 guilders.

In August of the same year Mozart returned to Prague and stayed initially in the inn The Three Golden Lions on the Coal Market (Uhelný trh 1). A commemorative plaque recalls his visit. He then moved into the Bertramka summer villa (today a museum, *see page 68*), the property of a musician named Dušeks and his wife, also a musician. Here he completed *Don Giovanni*, conducting the premiere himself at the Nostiz Theatre on 29 October 1787. It was a roaring success. He spent 1789 travelling backwards and forwards from Berlin, staying at Bertramka for a short period each time. It was here, in 1791, that he composed *La Clemenzia di Tito* in only 18 days; the opera also had its premiere in the Nostiz Theatre, on 6 September 1791. Three months later, Mozart died in poverty and almost forgotten in Vienna. In Prague, however, a requiem composed for the occasion was performed before a large congregation of mourners in the Church of St Nicholas in the Lesser Quarter.

Ludwig van Beethoven (1770–1827) visited Prague on several occasions. In 1796 he stayed in the Lesser Quarter in the inn The Golden Unicorn, the former Wolkenstein Palace (*see page 44*), at No 11 Lázeňská ulice, where there is a commemorative plaque.

Carl Maria von Weber (1786–1826) served as conductor at the Estates Theatre (*see page 48*) between 1813–6. He returned to the city on several occasions and was also married here in 1817 in the Church of St Henry.

Franz Liszt (1811–1886) lived on the Coal Market (Uhelny trh 11) between 1840 and 1846.

Czech music will remain linked for ever with the names of three of the world's greatest composers, Smetana, Dvořák and Janáček.

Bedřich Smetana (1824–84) spent most of his life in Prague. He lived at Železná ulice 548, on the corner of the Old Town square (commemorative plaque). One of his biggest preoccupations was the nature of an independent Czech popular opera, a matter which aroused the entire nation. He demanded a fully developed dramatic style which would do musical justice to the newly discovered melodic patterns of the Czech language, although this led to his being scorned as a 'Wagnerian' or 'Germaniser' by the Czech old guard, who preferred traditional melodies. In 1868, as the representative of all Czech artists, he laid the foundation stone of the National Theatre and conducted that same evening the premiere of his dramatic opera *Libuše*. He also gave the world the most frequently performed Czech opera, *The Bartered Bride*, as well as celebrating the countryside and history of his native land in the music cycle *My Fatherland*, whose most famous movement *The Moldau* continues to transfix the listener with its powerful emotions. Smetana died in the mental hospital at U Karlova 468. His grave is in the cemetery on the Vyšehrad (*see page 65*). A Smetana Museum (*see page 59*) has been set up in a house by the Vltava, near the Charles Bridge.

Antonín Dvořák (1841–1904) was the master of the symphony, chamber music and oratorio. Unlike Smetana, Dvořák attracted musical fame beyond the boundaries of his native land during his own lifetime. What paved the way for his international recognition was his cycle *Music From Moravia*, a radical interpretation of traditional folk songs. Aided by his friend Johannes Brahms, his first major triumph was in London, where his *Stabat Mater*

Bedřich Smetana

Dvořák Museum poster

At the Dvořák Museum

Concert in St Nicholas'

was rapturously received, followed by New York, Berlin, Vienna and Budapest. In 1891 Dvořák went to America as the director of the New York Conservatory, and it was here that he produced his most popular orchestral score, *Symphony No. 9 From the New World*. Dvořák left for posterity an impressive collection of compositions: 31 works of chamber music, 14 string quartets, 50 orchestral works and nine symphonies, such as the catchy melodies enshrined in his *Slavonic Dances*. Apart from his time in America, Dvořák lived most of his life in Prague. He died at his home in the Zitná ulice 14 (commemorative plaque). His grave is also on the Vyšehrad (*see page 65*). There is a Dvořák Museum in the Villa Amerika (*see page 66*).

Leoš Janáček (1854–1928), the third great Czech composer, lived almost all his life in Brno, but studied organ music in Prague for a while from 1874, and lived at Štěpánská ulice 50. Following on from Smetana and Dvořák, Janáček developed his own theory of the 'speech melody', according to which the melodic form followed the tone patterns of speech. He elevated this principle to one of the fundamentals of composition in his operas, the most famous of which are *The Cunning Little Vixen*, *Katja Kabanová* and *The House of the Dead*.

Concerts and festivals

Prague has three symphony orchestras and a number of chamber orchestras. The most famous concert hall in the city is the **Dvořák Hall** in the Rudolfinum by the Vltava (Náměsti Jan Palach). In the summer months, concerts are often held in churches and palaces.

The most important event in the musical calendar is the **Prague Spring** (Prasžské jaro), held every year from mid-May until early June, a music festival in which world-famous musicians participate. **Mozart's Prague** is another festival which attracts international orchestras to Prague, from mid-June to early July. In recent years, as a counterpart to the Prague Spring, the **Prague Winter** has been instituted (first week in January).

The concert season proper begins in mid-September, when the Czech Symphony Orchestra and the Prague Symphony Orchestra begin their cycle of concerts, which then run throughout the entire winter. Apart from the two orchestras and local soloists, the Prague winter season also includes a large number of famous instrumental ensembles and soloists (including jazz and pop musicians).

Theatre (divadlo)

It has been calculated that Paris possesses one theatre for every 90,000 inhabitants, and Berlin one for every 150,000. Prague, on the other hand, has a theatre for every 40,000 citizens; the city on the Vltava possesses, in fact, no fewer than 30 theatres attended by more than three million visitors each year.

There are three state-run theatres: the **National Theatre**, tel: 2491 3437; the **Estates Theatre**, tel: 2421 5001; and the **State Opera**: tel. 2422 7683, in which operas, ballets and plays are performed.

Among the best of the independent theatre venues are the following:

Theatre on the Balustrades (Divadlo na zábradlí), Anenské náměsti 5 (drama and mime; this is where Havel's plays were performed, tel: 2422 9517).

Archa Theatre (Divadlo Archa), Na Poriči 26, Prague 1, tel: 232 7570. Avant-garde theatre with visiting foreign performers.

Gag Studio Borise Hybnera, Národní třida 25, tel: 2422 9095. Mainly mime.

Franz Kafka Theatre, Celetná 17, Prague 1, tel: 232 8824. Devoted to the city's most famous writer.

Reduta, Národní třida 20, Prague 1, tel: 2491 2246. Contemporary drama as well as jazz and rock.

Laterna Magica, Národní třída 4. This Prague theatre is without doubt the one which is best known beyond the national boundaries, with its inimitable mixture of drama, film and ballet and unusual optical and acoustic effects. The actors appear to step from the stage directly into the film, and vice-versa; the 'polyecran technique' can be projected onto eight screens simultaneously.

In Prague there are also several puppet theatres, including the oldest and most traditional one, **Spejbla a Hurvinka**, Rimská 45 Prague 2, tel: 251 666; and the **National Marionette Theatre** (Národní divadlo marionet), Žatecká 1, Prague 1, tel: 232 3429.

The National Theatre

Laterna Magica theatre

Food and Drink

The menu in Prague restaurants may not be as varied as in other cities, but the food on offer is tasty and satisfying – albeit sometimes on the heavy side, for most dishes contain a large proportion of meat and very few vegetables.

Specialities

The most famous culinary speciality in Prague, indeed in Bohemia as a whole, is the dumpling (*knedlíky*), eaten above all with roast pork (*vepřová pečeně*), the favourite local dish, and served mostly with sauerkraut (*kyselé zelí*).

Popular hors d'oeuvres include sardines (*sardinky*), pâté (*paštika*), garnished herring (*sled's přilohou*), cold meat (*studené maso*) and tongue in aspic (*jazyk v rosolu*).

The most popular soup (*polévky*) is undoubtedly the Bohemian potato soup (*bramboračka* or *bramborová polévka*), whose principal ingredients are boiled potatoes and mushrooms. Another favourite is beef soup (*hovězi polévka*). Soups of many kinds are served and some are almost a meal in themselves.

As far as fish dishes (*masité pokrmy*) are concerned, carp (*kapr*) cooked in a variety of ways is the most popular; it is eaten in virtually every household at Christmas. Trout (*pstruh*) is also frequently available.

Favourite meat dishes, apart from roast pork, are beef (*hovězi maso*), loin of beef/fillet of beef (*svíčová pečeně*), braised beef (*dušená svícková*), goulash (*guláš*), steak (*biftek*), tongue (*jazyk*), escalope of veal (*videňský řízek*), roast veal (*teleci pečeně*), beef olives (*ruláda*), smoked meat (*uzené maso*), smoked sausage (*uzenka*) and the famous Prague ham (*pražska šunka*). Hot frankfurter-type sausages (*párky*) and fried sausages (*klobása*) are sold on the streets until late at night.

Prague ham for sale

Game and poultry are also popular, especially goose (*husa*) and roast duck (*kachna na roštu*), mostly served with dumplings and sauerkraut.

A great local speciality in Prague are the many desserts. Here, too, dumplings are the main favourites, filled with plums (*švestky*), sweet cherries (*třešně*), morello cherries (*višně*) or apricots (*meruňky*). Another popular dessert is pancakes (*palačinka*). There are also a variety of local cakes, many of which, however, are very sweet.

Drinks

Czech beer *(pivo)* is probably the finest in the world. Its quality is largely thanks to the famous hops, which have been cultivated in Northern Bohemia ever since the Middle Ages. The principal hop centre is Žatec (Saaz). In Prague both light (*svetlé*) as well as dark (*tmavé* or *černé*) beer is available.

Enjoying a beer in the square

Pilsen beer
Wine bar on Slavony

The most famous beers are *Pilsener Urquell* from Plzen (Pilsen), *Budvar* from České Budějovice (Budweis) and *Zlatý Bazant* (Golden Pheasant), the renowned Slovak beer. The beer from Prague's Smíchov brewery is also very good, and then there is the strong dark beer brewed on the premises at U Fleků. Another strong beer is Bránické from the Prague district of Braník.

The wine bars, known as *vinárna*, serve predominantly Czech wines. The best wine (*víno*) comes from Žernoseky in the Elbe Valley, where the Melník wines are also cultivated. Good wines are also produced in Southern Moravia, in places like Mikulov, Hodonin, Znojmo or Valtice. Red is *červené,* white is *bilé.*

One kind of national drink is undoubtedly the 40–60 percent plum schnapps (*Sliwowitz/ slivovice*), and the bitters from Carlsbad, known as *Becherovka*, are also very popular.

Selected restaurants

Lesser Quarter

Valdstejnská hospoda (Waldstein Inn), Valdštejnské nám., Prague 1, tel: 536 195. At the foot of Hradčany. Traditional decor, game specialities, not expensive.

U tři pštrosů, Dražického nám. 12, Prague 1, tel: 2451 0761. Next to the Charles Bridge. Traditional decor and Bohemian cuisine, upper price range.

U čerta, Nerudova 4, Prague 1, tel: 530 975. Stylish, with waiters who speak English. Reasonably priced.

U Malfrů, Maltézské nám. 11, Prague 1, tel: 24 51 0296. French restaurant since 1543, French prices.

Nebozízek, Petřínské sady 411, Prague 1, tel: 537 905. At the middle station of the funicular up Petřín Hill. Large terrace, with a view of the Vltava and the Old Town.

Old Town

Café Nouveau, Náměsti Republiky 5, tel: 232 3764. On the ground floor of The Municipal House. Simple inexpensive meals, wonderful art nouveau decor.

Na Přikopě, Na Přikopě 17, tel: 2421 0661. Good traditional food and reasonable prices.

Parnas, Smetanovo nábřeži 2, Prague 1, tel: 242 276 14. Expensive. Still among the very best restaurants in the city, and its view of the castle is divine.

Pivince Skořepce, Skořepka 1, Prague 1, tel: 242 147. Traditional atmosphere, reasonably priced.

Praha Tamura, Havelská 6, Prague 1, tel: 2423 2056. Expensive. Superb Japanese sushi and sashimi.

Opera Grill, Karoliny Světlé 35, tel: 265 508. International cuisine, authentic old-fashioned decor.

Zlatá ulička (Golden Lane), Masná 9, Prague 1, tel: 232 884. Moderate. Yugoslav specialties in a tiny café.

New Town

Kavarna Velryba, Opatovická 24, tel: 24 91 23 91. Comfortable, inexpensive, fun but smoky.

Radost FX Café, Bělehradská 120, tel: 25 12 100. A rarity in Prague, a good vegetarian restaurant.

Vltava, Rasinovo nábreží (right bank of the Vltava where the cruisers pull in), tel: 29 49 64. Terrace on the Vltava. Reasonably priced and generous portions.

International specialities

Ali Baba, Vodičkova 5, Prague 1, tel: 2491 2084. Moderate. All sorts of Arabic treats.

Bella Napoli, V jámě 8, Prague 1, tel: 2422 7315. Moderate. Moravian and Italian wines.

Buffalo Bill's, Vodičkova 9, Prague 1, tel: 2421 5479. Moderate. Wide variety of Tex-Mex favorites, spicy without being fiery.

Country Life, Jungmannova 1, Prague 1, tel: 2419 1739. Also, Melantrichova 15, Prague 1, tel: 2421 3366. Inexpensive. Standing room only for simple vegetarian pizza, salads, sandwiches.

Dolly Bell, Neklanova 20, Prague 2, tel: 29 88 15. Moderate. Delicious Yugoslav dishes in a stylish restaurant.

Jewish Restaurant, Maiselova 18, Prague 1. Inexpensive/moderate. Kosher meals.

Kongzi, Seifertova 18, Prague 3, tel: 27 50 26. Moderate. Chinese food so spicy it'll bring tears to your eyes.

La Palma, Na hrázi 32, Prague 8, tel: 683 2764. Moderate. Continues to hold its own as one of the most popular Italian restaurants in town.

Savarin, Prague 1, Na příkopě 10, tel: 22 20 66.

Pizzeria Kmotra, V Jirchářích 12, Prague 1, tel: 2491 5809. Inexpensive/moderate. Popular with both locals and foreigners.

The Jewish Restaurant

87

Art nouveau embellishment

Coffee time

A healthy alternative

Red Hot and Blues, Jakubská 12, Prague 1, tel: 231 4639. Moderate. New Orleans style cooking, live jazz.

Rotisserie, Mikulandská 6, Prague 1, tel: 2491 2334. Moderate. Steak and fish, extensive wine list.

Sate, Pohořelec 152/3 , Prague 1, tel: 532 113. Near the castle. Inexpensive. Indonesian specialties.

U Cedru, Na Hutích 13, Prague 6, tel: 312 2974. Moderate. Very good Lebanese food.

U Maltézských rytířů, Prokopská 10, Prague 1, tel: 536 357, 536 650. Moderate. Try the apple strudel.

V Zátiši, Lililová 1, Prague 1, tel: 2422 8977. Expensive. Delectable main courses include beef Wellington.

Bohemian specialities

Černý kůň (The Black Horse), Štepánská 61, Prague 2, tel: 2421 2659. Inexpensive/moderate. Traditional cuisine.

Česká restaurace (Czech Restaurant), Krakovská 63, Prague 1, tel: 2421 6935. Inexpensive. Good pub food.

Na Zvonarce, Šafaříkova 1, Prague 2, tel: 254 534. Inexpensive. Good Czech cooking, large pub restaurant, great views from the summer terrace.

Nebozizek (The Auger), Petřínské sady 411, Prague 1, tel: 537 905. Moderate. Nice view of the castle.

Quido, Kubelíkova 22, Prague 3, tel: 270 950. Inexpensive/moderate. Well-prepared traditional Czech meals.

U Benedikta, Benediktská 11, Prague 1, tel: 231 1527. Inexpensive. Standard Czech fare, but done well.

U Buldoka (The Bulldog), Presova 1, Prague 5, tel: 534 638. Inexpensive. Good, standard pub food without too much smoky pub atmosphere.

U Čízků, Karlovo nám. 34, Prague 2, tel: 298 891. Moderate. Traditional Bohemian dinners.

U Kalicha (The Chalice), Na Bojišti 14, Prague 2, tel: 290 701. Moderate.

U Matouše, Preslova 17, Prague 5, tel: 546 284/541 877. Inexpensive. Imaginative menu offers traditional Bohemian and inventive new combinations. The roast duck is worth the 24-hours advance notice.

U městské knihovny (City Library), Valentinská 11, Prague 1, tel: 231 0867. Inexpensive/moderate. Typical pub-restaurant, tastier than average Czech fare.

U pastýřky (The Shepherdess), Bělehradská 15, Prague 4, tel: 434 093. Moderate. Delicious Slovak food and authentic atmosphere in backwoods-style cabin; large beer garden in front.

Velryba (The Whale), Opatovická 24, Prague 1, tel: 2491 2391. Inexpensive/moderate. Hipster haunt. Good Czech fare, café drinks, inexpensive pasta dishes.

Vinárna U knížků, Doksanská 20, Prague 8, tel: 684 6795. Inexpensive. Good basic Bohemian cooking in a family-run establishment.

Taverns (beer halls)

U dvou kocek (The Two Cats), Uhelný trh 10, Prague 1, tel: 2422 9982. One of the most popular of Prague's pubs: Pilsener Urquell.

U Fleků, Křemencova 11, Prague 1, tel: 2491 5118. The malthouse and brewery date from 1459. 13° dark beer still brewed on the premises, accompanied by traditional Prague cabaret.

U-Fleků tavern

U medvídků (The Bears), Na Peřstýně 7, Prague 1, tel: 2421 1916. This traditional restaurant offers Southern Bohemian and Old Czech specialities, accompanied by 12° Budvar.

U Pinkasů, Jungmannovo nám. 15, Prague 1, tel: 2423 0828. This establishment has been pulling Pilsener Urquell since 1843.

U sv. Tomáše (St Thomas's), Letenská 12, Prague 1, tel: 531 632. 12° beer from Braník.

Bránický Formanka, Vodičkova 26, Prague 1, tel: 260 005. 14° beer from Braník.

Černý Pivovar (Black Brewery), Karlovo nám. 15, Prague 2, tel: 29 44 51. 12° Pilsener Urquell.

Plzeňský dvůr, Milady Horakové 59, Prague 7, tel: 37 11 50. 12° Pilsener Urquell.

U Bonaparta, Nerudova 29, Prague 1, tel: 531 684. 12° beer from Smíchov.

U Černého vola (The Black Bull), Loretánské nám. 1, Prague 1 tel: 53 86 37. 12° beer from Velké Popovice.

U dvou srdcí (Two Hearts), U lužického semináře 38, Prague 1, tel: 536 597. 12° Pilsener Urquell.

U Schnellů, Tomášská 2, Prague 1, tel: 532 004. 12° Pilsener Urquell.

U zlatého tygra (The Golden Tiger), Husova 17, Prague 1, tel: 2422 9020. 12° Pilsener Urquell.

Wine Bars

Blatnice, Michalská 8, Prague 1, tel: 263 812. Moravian wines from the area around Blatnice.

Klašterní vinárna (Monastery Wine Bar), Národní 8, Prague 1, tel: 290 596. In the former Ursuline Convent, serving wines from Moravia and Nitra.

Lobkovická vinárna, Vlašská 17, Prague 1, tel: 530 185. A historic wine bar in the Lesser Quarter; wines from Melník are served here.

Makarská, Malostranské nam. 2, tel: 531 573. Balkan wines and specialities.

Nebozízek, Petřínské sady, Prague 5, tel: 537 905. Reached the funicular from the Lesser Quarter, with an impressive view of Prague and Hradčany.

Parnas Restaurant

Parnas, Prague 1, Smetanovo nábřeží 2, tel: 265 017. International cuisine with a fine view of the Hradčany.

Svatá Klara (St Clare), Prague 7, U trojského zámku 9, tel: 841 213. Exclusive cellar wine bar at the entrance to Prague Zoo.

U labutí (The Swans), Hradčanské nám. 11, Prague 1, tel: 5 9 476. Exclusive wine bar near the castle serving South Moravian wines.

U mecenáše (The Sponsor), Malostranské nám. 10, Prague 1, tel: 533 881. There was an inn in the house at the sign of the Golden Lion as long ago as 1604.

U patrona (The Patron), Dražického nám. 4, Prague 1, tel: 531 661. Cosy atmosphere, South Moravian wine.

U pavouka (The Spider), Prague 1, Celetná 17, tel: 231 8714. This historic wine bar with its Gothic and Renaissance halls serves wines from Southern Moravia.

U zelené záby (The Green Frog), U radnice 8, Prague 1, tel: 2422 8133. This institution has poured wine from Velké Žernoseky in Bohemia since the 15th century.

U zlaté konvice (The Golden Pot), Melantrichova 20, Prague 1, tel: 2422 78 85. Wine bar in cellars whose walls date from the 14th century; wines from Valtice.

U zlatého jelena (The Golden Stag), Celetná 11, Prague 1, tel: 268 595. Cellar wine bar with wines from Southern Moravia.

Art Nouveau coffee house

Coffee Houses

The Prague coffee house remains an important element in the daily life of the city. The coffee is not always very strong but the atmosphere is good.

Arco, Prague 1, Hybernská 16.

Café Milena, Staroměstské nám., Prague 1.

Evropa, Václavské nám. 29, Prague 1.

Gany's, Národní 20, Prague 1.

Globe Coffee House, Janovského, Prague 1.

Pilha Café, Klimentská 2, Prague 1.

Velryba, Opatovická 24, Prague 1.

Café Arco

Nightlife

Prague by night

In view of the limited space available, it is only possible to list here a selection of the city's wide range of cultural activities and nightlife. More detailed information is obtainable from the Prague Information Service (*see page 98*) which also publishes an English edition of their calendar of events.

Jazz, rock and pop

AghaRTA Jazz Centrum, Krakovská 5, Prague 1. Expect to hear the best live jazz in town.

Barclub, Hybernská 10, Prague 1. A hole in the wall with excellent acoustics for reggae. DJs speak English if you have a request.

Újezd, Újezd 18, Prague 1. Formerly the Borát, which was the unofficial centre for Prague's illegal music scene. Attracts metal bands from across Europe.

Bunkr, Lodecká 2, Prague 1. Can be terrific or lame. This was the first rock club in the new Czech Republic.

Junior klub, Koněvova 219, Prague 3. Hosts the best of the Czech alternative scene. Bring an open mind.

Legenda, Křižovnická 12, Prague 1. Grunge club mixes ABBA with Nirvana. Tequila is the drink of choice.

Reduta, Národní 20, Prague 1. Long-running home of great jazz in Prague.

Rock Café, Národní 20, Prague 1. Excellent Czech and foreign bands.

Roxy, Dlouhá 33, Prague 1. Artsy club hangout.

Uzi Biker, Legerova 44, Prague 2. Wannabe club. In-house tattoo artist does good business.

Viola Jazz Club, Národní třída 7, Prague 1. Only open for jazz on Saturday nights, this classy joint hosts the bands who frequent Reduta and AghaRTA Jazz Centrum.

Jazz in Staré Město

Národní třída – clubland

Party time in Prague

Getting There

By air

Prague is firmly on the international air grid and is directly linked to virtually every European capital, including London, from where the flight time is only 1½ hours. Many airlines fly from New York to Prague and in the case of the ČSA, the Czech national carrier, the flight is nonstop. ČSA also flies from Chicago via Montreal as well as from Toronto. There are now a few charter flights available and it is worthwhile checking availability with travel agents.

Prague Ruzyně airport lies 20km (13 miles) northwest of the city. There are public bus services to the centre, as well as taxi and hire cars. The state travel agency Čedok runs a shuttle bus service between the airport and the city's Interhotels between 11am and 4pm. ČSA also operates a similar service between the airport and the city terminal. It runs every 30 minutes, Monday to Friday 5.30am–6.30pm, Saturday and Sunday 6.30am–6.30pm. The journey takes 30 minutes and costs a nominal sum. The buses also stop at the terminal station Dejvická of the green Metro line A.

Opposite: Prague's main railway station

BA arrival

93

By rail

There is no through service from the channel ports. The service from Paris is known to the French as the Paris–Praha Express and to the Czechs as the Zapadní Express. It leaves from the Gare de l'Est at 11pm and goes via Frankfurt and Nuremberg, arriving in Prague shortly before 6pm the following day. There are direct train connections to Prague from Germany and Austria. From Stuttgart and Munich, the journey takes approximately 8 hours, from Frankfurt 10 hours, Berlin 6 hours, Hamburg 14 hours and Vienna 6 hours. All trains from Southern Germany and Austria come in at the main Wilsonova Station (Hlavní nádraží). Trains from Berlin come into the Masaryk Station (Masarykovo nádraží) or at Prague-Holesovice Station. The Wilsonova station is clearly laid out on two floors. The lower level contains the counters for domestic tickets as well as the PIS information office and shops. International tickets are purchased in the upper hall, which also has the accomodation booking agency and exchange bureau, AVE.

Taxis line up outside the southern side exit.

Domestic and international tickets can be purchased in Czech crowns, Western currency or by credit card at **Čedok**, Na příkopě 18, Prague 1, or from the railway station in crowns.

Further information about rail travel can be obtained from the main station in English, French or German, tel: 2421 7654; or from Holešovice station, tel: 2461 5865.

The Wilsonova Station

By car

Prague is easily accessible by car from western Europe. Most visitors will approach the Czech Republic from either Austria or Germany. The main border crossings are as follows:

Nuremberg via Waidhaus/Rozvadov (171 km/106 miles).

Munich via Bayrisch Eisenstein/Železná Rudá (171 km/106 miles).

Berlin via Zinnwald/Cínovecb (90 km/55 miles).

If you're entering Czechoslovakia from Austria:

Salzburg via Linz Summerau/Horni Dvořistě (186 km/115 miles)

Vienna via Gmünd/České Velenice (195 km/120 miles) or Grametten/Nová Bystřice (177 km/110 miles).

Drivers will require vehicle registration papers, a valid driving licence and a nationality sticker, and green card insurance is recommended. Drivers must be over the age of 21. The normal rules of the road apply; the maximum speed limit on country roads is 90kph/56mph, on motorways and major trunk roads it is 110kph/68mph, and in built-up areas 60kph/37mph. Seat belts must be worn and there is a general ban on driving while under the influence of alcohol.

Although there is an organised breakdown service including over 31 emergency aid vehicles in the country, it is often difficult to obtain the necessary spare parts for foreign vehicles.

It is advisable to obtain international travel insurance before starting your trip.

The agency **Yellow Angels**, a nonstop emergency for tourists and motorised visitors, can be reached by calling (02) 123. They normally have on hand people who speak English or German or at least can give you directions to the next garage.

Skodas are not extinct

Getting Around

Parking

Hradčany and Wenceslas Square and the surrounding streets, as well as large sections of the Old Town, are closed to motor traffic (except for access for hotel guests). In the city centre only cars with official permits may be parked. Public car parks (fee-paying) can be found near the National Theatre, the main railway station, beside the Vltava in the vicinity of the Hotel Intercontinental, between Masaryk Station and the Vltava promenade and near the larger hotels. Illegally parked vehicles are frequently towed away or clamped; information can be obtained at the nearest police station.

Dangers of illegal parking

Public Transport

The various means of public transport are cheap and well synchronised. The network includes trams and buses, the Metro and the funicular up the Petřín Hill. Tickets can be purchased in shops, at the kiosks of the Prague Public Transport Executive and from the automatic ticket machines at the stops or stations. Tickets cost a flat rate, and must be cancelled inside the trams and buses and before

THE PRAGUE METRO

entering the underground, where the cancelling machines are located directly at the entrance. There are no ticket or cancelling machines on the platforms, so even if you have no change make sure that you buy a ticket from the guard at the entrance and have it cancelled before you go through. On the underground these tickets allow you to change as often as you like within a 90-minute period, as long as you don't leave a station; with buses and trams you have to cancel a new ticket every time you get in.

Tram near Wencelas Square

There is also a special tourist ticket which allows an unlimited number of journeys within a set period of between 2 and 5 days. Transport on the entire network is completely free for children under 10 and adults over 70. Children under 16 only pay half fare. For ticket sales and further information contact the information office of the Public Transport Executive at Palackého nám. 8, tel: 264 682, or in the Můstek metro station exit in Jungmannovo nám. 1, tel: 2422 5135 (daily 7am–9pm)

The Prague Metro

The modern underground system links the centre with the suburbs and provides for convenient changes inside the city. It is a remarkably clean and quick means of public transport. The three lines have been developed with an eye towards expediency and by transferring it is possible to reach just about all the important tourist attractions located within the city.

Staroměstská Metro

The lines intersect at three main stations. From Můstek station at the bottom of Wenceslas Square you can take the green Line A over to the Lesser Quarter and Hradčany. The yellow Line B runs south to Charles Square and to the Smichovské nádraži station. The Florenc bus station and the northeast can be reached by travelling in the opposite direction. Line A intersects with the red Line C at the Muzeum station at the upper end of Wenceslas Square. The latter runs north to the main station, then to the Florenc bus station where it intersects with Line B before continuing to the terminus Nádraží Holesovice, the railway station for the majority of the trains on the Berlin to Budapest route. To the south it leads down to Vysehrad. Because of the frequency of the trains (every 5–12 minutes), you need plan for little more than 30 minutes even for journeys out into the suburbs. The Metro operates from 5am to midnight.

The green 'M' signs outside the stations are small and decidedly inconspicuous. But inside, the stations, often beautifully designed, are clean and clearly laid out. Network plans are prominently located at all entrances and above the platforms; the station you are at is highlighted; the stations you can change at are marked with the colour of the intersecting line.

Trams and buses

Tram line 22

Prague has a comprehensive bus route network: buses (autobus) and trolley buses (*Trolejbus*) run all day, particularly frequently in the suburbs, to connect with the Metro.

Among the many tram and bus routes within Prague, Line 22 is probably the most interesting for visitors. It runs from Náměstí Míru over Charles Square and along the Národní třída (National Street). It crosses the Vltava and then runs along the Karmelitská in the Lesser Quarter to the Lesser Quarter Square. From there it winds its way up the castle hill and on along the Keplerova to the starting point for Strahov and Petřín Hill. On Line 22 it is possible to have an almost complete tour of the city for only a few crowns. This is an ideal way of making first acquaintances with many of the sights.

Stall on Charles Bridge

Sightseeing and excursions

During the summer months, the tram offers the possibility of a sightseeing tour of the city along two different routes (lines 91 and 92). You can board, for example, by the main railway station, the National Theatre, or on the Malostranská náměstí in the Lesser Quarter.

A number of travel agents, including ČEDOK, organise sightseeing tours and excursions by coach. Departures are from the coach park at Bílkova 6 (opposite the Hotel Intercontinental).

Looking for inspiration

Apart from these regular tours there are also special tours organised around a central theme, including 'Romanesque Prague', 'Gothic Prague', 'The Prague of the Renaissance', 'The Prague of the Baroque Era', 'Musical Prague', etc. Popular one-day excursions to destinations outside the city include 'The Castles and Palaces of Bohemia', 'Castles and Palaces along the Vltava', 'Pearls of Bohemian Gothic' and 'To the beauty spots of Southern Bohemia'.

Facts for the Visitor

Passports and visas

For citizens of most European countries as well as the United States and Canada, no visa is required. Nationals of other countries are advised to contact their respective Czech embassies or consulates for information.

Customs

The Czech customs controls are quite rigid. In order to avoid misunderstandings, you should check on anything you're unsure about beforehand. Upon entering the country, you'll be given a leaflet explaining the customs regulations. Note that antiques more than 50 years old can only be taken out with a special permit, which can be very difficult to obtain.

ČSA (national airline)

United Kingdom: 12a Margaret Street, London W1N 7LF, tel: 0171-255 1898 or 255 1366.

United States: 545 Fifth Avenue, New York, NY 10017, tel: 212-682 7541 or 682 5833.

In Prague: Tickets and reservations: Revoluční 1 (next to Kotva) Prague 1, tel: 2421 0132. Flight information: Revoluční 25 (Vltava) Prague 1, tel: 231 7395/2146. Both are located near the Metro station Náměstí Republiky.

Central information, Ruzyně Airport, tel: 334 1111.

Čedok (national travel agency)

United Kingdom, Čedok London Limited, Czechoslovak Travel Bureau, 17–18 Old Bond Street, London W1X 4RB, tel: 0171- 629 6058. fax: 017-1 493 7841.

Browsing for antiques

USA, Čedok, Czechoslovak Travel Bureau Inc., 10 East 40th Street, New York, NY 10016, 1-212 609 9720. Fax 1-212 418 0597.

In Prague:ČEDOK, Na příkopě 18, tel: 2419 7111. Abundant information for tourists can also be obtained from the **Prague Information Service** located at Staroměstské nám. (Old Town Square), Prague 1, tel: 2421 2844/5; at Na příkopě 20, tel: 544 444; and at the Hradčanská metro station.

Further travel agencies and tour agencies

Here is a list of the principal, established agencies, although new private enterprises are being established all the time:

Autoturist, Prague 2, Na rybníčku 16, Prague 3, tel: 2422 2746; Prague 10, Limuzská 12, tel: 773 455.

AVE , Wilsonova Station, Prague 2, tel: 2422 3226.

Adco Travel Agency, Bilkova 19, tel: 6631 0061.

American Express, Vaclauske nam. 56 (Wenceslas Square), tel: 2421 5397.

Bohemia Travel, Zlatnická 7, Prague 1, tel: 232 3877.

Čedok, Na příkopě 18, tel: 2419 7111; Bilkova 6, 231 8255; Rytiřská 16, tel: 235 6356.

Mantin Tours, Rokoko Arcade, Václavské nám., tel: 2421 5018.

Pragotour, Prague 1, U Obecního domů 2, tel: 2325 1128.

Wittmann Tours, Uruguayská 7, tel: 439 6293.

Currency and exchange

The national unit of currency is the Czech crown (koruna), for which the abbreviation is Kčs. It is subdivided into 100 halér, abbreviated to h. Coins are in circulation to the value of 5, 10, 20, and 50 halér and 1, 2, 5, and 10 crowns. Banknotes are issued to the value of 10, 20, 50, 100, 500 and 1,000 crowns.

There are no restrictions on importing or exporting freely convertible currencies, but crowns cannot be taken in or out of the country. Money can be changed in banks, travel agents, hotels and at exchange offices, which are often open during the evening and at weekends (especially those in the main railway station, in Wenceslas Square, Na příkopě and Staroměstské nám.). Eurocheques are widely accepted in the Czech Republic, and international credit cards are becoming more and more acceptable by large hotels, restaurants, and shops catering to tourists, but it is wise to check in advance.

Service charges and tips

A service charge is included in bills issued by hotels and restaurants in Prague. An additional tip (approximately 10 percent of the total charge) is customary.

Keeping guard

Shopping

For tourists, the most interesting shopping streets are in the Old Town (Staré Město): Na příkopě, Wenceslas Square (Václavské náměstí), Národni trída and the surrounding alleys. Department stores still offer predominantly local goods produced to traditional designs, but there are already a large number of smaller shops offering a wider range of items more in accordance with western tastes. Bohemia glass items and china are available in a particularly wide variety of attractive designs.

Traditional chemist's

Opening times

No shortage of information

Shops are usually open Monday to Friday from 8.30am –6pm (sometimes with a midday break), and on Saturday until noon. An increasing number of shops in Prague open on Thursday until 8pm as well as on Saturday and Sunday afternoon.

Shops in the centre, selling goods of particular interest to tourists, often remain open until late in the evening in summer. Most museums are closed on Monday.

Post

The main post office is near Wenceslas Square (Václavské nám.), in the Jindřišská ul. 14. It is open 24 hours a day. Postboxes are orange or blue. Telegrams can be sent from post offices or by dialling 127. To make an international call, dial 00 + the international code: Australia 61; France 33; Germany 49; Japan 81; Netherlands 31; Spain 34; United Kingdom 44; US and Canada 1.

Telephone

It is usually easiest to make calls from a post office, as many public phones are out of order.

Important telephone numbers

Emergency: tel: 155
Emergency dental service: Vladislavova 22, Prague 1, tel: 2422 7663.
Police: tel: 158
Fire brigade: tel. 150
Lost property: Karolíny sřetté 5, Prague 1, tel: 2422 6133.

Travellers with disablities

Czech Association of Persons with Disabilities, Karlinské nám., 12, tel: 2421 5915.
Union of the Disabled, Konviktská 6, tel: 2422 7203.

Diplomatic representation

United Kingdom, Thunovská 14, Prague 1, tel: 224 510 439, 533 370.
USA, Tržiste 15, Prague 1, tel: 536 6416.

Accommodation

Steeply rising numbers of visitors and a lack of hotel accommodation (although it is increasing) mean that advance reservations are strongly recommended.

The list below gives a number of recommended hotels, ranging from the luxury to cheap categories.

$$$$$

Esplanade, Washingtonova 19, Prague 1, tel: 2421 1715, fax: 2422 9306; **Inter-Continental**, Náměstí Curieových 5, Prague 1, tel: 2488 1111; **Jalta**, Václavské nám. 45, Prague 1, tel: 2422 9133; **Palace**, Panská 12, Prague 1, tel: 2409 3111, fax: 2422 1240; **Prague**, Susická 20, Prague 6, tel: 2434 2650, fax: 2431 1218; **Hotel Savoy**, Keplerova 6, Prague 1, tel: 2430 2111, fax: 2430 2128.

The Inter-Continental

$$$$

Prague Penta Renaissance, Celnici 7, Prague 1, tel: 2481 0396, fax: 231 3133; **Grand Hotel Bohemia**, Královodvorská 4, Prague 1, tel: 232 3417, fax: 232 9545; **Best Western Meteor Plaza**, Hybernská 6, Prague 1, tel: 2419 2111, fax 2422 0681; **Hotel Hoffmeister**, Pod Bruskou, Prague 1, tel: 561 8155, 2451 1015, fax: 530 959; **Adria**, Václavské nám. 26, Prague 1, tel: 2421 6543, fax: 2421 1025; **Ambassador**, Václavské nám. 5, Prague 1, tel: 2419 3111; **Atlantik**, Na Poříčí 9, Prague 1, tel: 231 8512; **Atrium**, Pobřežni 1, Prague 8, tel: 2484 1111, fax: 2481 1937; **Diplomat**, Evropská 15, Prague 6, tel: 2439 4111, fax: 34 1 7 31. **Forum**, Kongressová 4, Prague 4, tel: 6119 1111, fax: 420 684. **Olympik**, Sokolovská 138, Prague 8, tel: 6618 1111, fax: 6631 0559. **Panaroma**, Milevská 7, Prague 4, tel: 6116 1111, fax: 426 263. **Paříž**, Obecního domu 1, Prague 1, tel: 2422 2151, fax: 2422 5475. **President**, Nám. Curieových 100, Prague 1, tel: 231 7523, fax: 231 8247.

101

$$$

Ametyst, Jana Masaryka 11, Prague 2, tel: 691 1758, fax: 691 1790; **Axa**, Na Poříčí 40, Prague 1, tel: 2481 2580; **Belvedere**, Milady Horakové 19, Prague 7, tel: 374 741; **Beránek**, Kubanské nám. 6, Prague 10, tel: 749 645; **Evropa**, Václavské náměstí 25, Prague 1, tel: 2422 8117, 2421 4074; **Flora**, Vinohradská 121, Prague 3, tel: 278 981; **Golf**, Plzeňská 215a, Prague 5, tel: 523 251; **Karl-Inn**, Šaldova 54, Prague 8, tel: 2481 1718; fax: 2481 2681; **Moráň**, Na Moráni 15, Prague 2, tel: 2491 5208, fax: 297 533; **Poseidon**, Vyskočilova 741/3, Prague 4, tel: 692 3396, fax: 692 3394; **Union**, Ostrčilovo nám. 4, Prague 2, tel: 6121 4812, fax: 6121 4820; **U tří pštrosů**, Dražického nám. 12, Prague 1, tel: 2451 0779, fax: 2451 0783;

$$

Balkan, Svornosti 28, Prague 5, tel: 540 777; **Central**, Rybná 8, Prague 1, tel: 2481 2041; **Hybernia**, Hybernská 24 Prague 1, tel: 2421 0439; **Junior hotel**, Zitná 12. Prague 2, tel: 2491 5767; **Juventus**, Blanická 10, Prague 2, tel: 255 151; **Merkur**, Těšnov 9, tel: 232 3906, 2481 0933; **Michle**, Nuselská 124, Prague 4, tel: 426 024; **Opera**, Těšnov 13, Prague 1, tel: 231 5735; **Ostaš**, Orebitská 8, Prague 3,tel: 627 9418; **Madape**, Malešická 74, Prague 3, tel: 771 3355, fax: 771 355; **Praga**, Plzeňská 29, Prague 5, tel: 2451 1742; **Transit**, Ruzyňská 197, Prague 6, tel: 367 769; **U Blaženky**, U Blaženky 1, Prague 5, tel: 245 1105.

Youth Hostels

For information about youth hostels, contact: **CKM**, Žitná 10, Nové Město, tel: 292 984; **Junior Hotel**, Žitná 12, Nové Město, tel: 249 157/67.

Camp sites

Information regarding camping is available through automobile associations or the headquarters of the Czech Automobile Association: **Autoturist**, Na Rybíčku, 16, Prague 2, tel: 2422 2746. Open: Monday to Friday 9am–noon, 1pm–4pm.

ABC Autocamp, Za Mlýnem, Prague 4, tel: 460 226.

Caravan, Prague 9, Kbely, Mladoboleslavská 27, tel: 892 532. May to October.

Caravancamp, Prague 5, Plzeňská, tel: 524 714. March to October.

Dolní Chabry, Prague 8 – Dolní Chabry, Ústecká ul. June to September.

Kotva, Prague 4, U ledáren 55, tel: 461 712. Open May to September.

Mejto, Prague 10 – Nedveží, Rokytná 84, tel: 750 312-5. Open year-round.

Sportcamp, Prague 5, V podhájí, tel: 521 802. March to October.

TJ Aritma, Prague 6, Nad lávkou 3, tel: 368 351. April to October.

Private lodgings

Private lodgings offer a comparatively inexpensive alternative to hotel rooms. They can be booked through a number of travel agencies, both in Prague and overseas, including the following addresses in the UK: **The Czechbook**, 52 St John's Park, London SE3 7JP, tel: 0181- 853 1168; **Czechdays**, 89 Valence Road, Lewis, Sussex BN7 1SJ, tel: 0273- 474 738. It's also usually possible to find something suitable even at the last minute. Private people advertise accommodation on the street corners.

Index